JOHN FISHER'S MAGIC BOOK

by John Fisher

illustrations by Tomie de Paola

PRENTICE-HALL, INC., Englewood Cliffs, N.J.

John Fisher's Magic Book by John Fisher
First published in the U.S.A., 1971, by Prentice-Hall,
Inc., Englewood Cliffs, N.J.

First published in Great Britain, 1968
Copyright © by John Fisher, 1968
Copyright © by Prentice-Hall, Inc., 1971, for
illustrations in this edition

ISBN-0-13-510206-5
ISBN-0-13-510222-7 p6k.
Library of Congress Catalog Card Number: 70-146962
Printed in the United States of America · J

Prentice-Hall International, Inc., London
Prentice-Hall of Australia, Pty. Ltd., Sydney
Prentice-Hall of Canada, Ltd., Toronto
Prentice-Hall of India Private Ltd., New Delhi
Prentice-Hall of Japan, Inc., Tokyo

10   9   8   7   6   5

Dedicated to Denis Yetman,
the first guide in the labyrinth

A Preface to Mystery

This book is a MAGIC BOOK, by which I mean not a book about magic and its secrets, but a book designed, however weird and fascinating the idea may sound, to play the part of a magician. To enjoy this unique form of literary entertainment, you have merely to turn to a trick (I prefer to call them "swindles" actually!), gather together the necessary props as detailed at the beginning of the item, sit back, relax, and then follow the instructions carefully. You will then see some bewildering and inextricable happening, some flabbergasting climax evolve right before your eyes and in your very own hands.

Here you will find the whole vast panorama of modern sorcery represented by some 74 "swindles" ranging from vanishing tricks to penetrations, escapology to mind-reading experiments, metamorphosis to comedy conjuring. There is even some juggling and, not least worthy of being styled amazing, a number of everyday impossibilities that I know for certain you have never considered to be impossible before! What you will not find, however, are the secrets, those subtle, inward workings to which the magician owes so much. So decorously does this book live up to its reputation as a true magician!

Have fun, and remember, it's a "Fishy Business," this Magic!

John Fisher.

Acknowledgment

Even if conjuring can be defined as the apparent accomplishment of the impossible, the magician still cannot solve the one impossibility inherent in conjuring itself, that of tracing back each individual trick to the most significant stage in its development. All conjuring technique is evolved from seven basic principles with ultimate roots themselves in the earliest of times. Hence the impossibility of giving credit exactly where it is due.

It is possible however to acknowledge my mentors in the above inextricable and indefinable traditions, namely, in alphabetical order; R. M. Abraham, Wizard Edward Beal, Arthur Bridgeman, Lewis Carroll, Fitch Cheney, Henry Christ, Paul Curry, Victor Eigen, Alexander Elmsley, Martin Gardner, Robert Harbin, Royal Vale Heath, Bob Hummer, Stewart James, R. M. Jamison, Stewart Judah, Harry Lorayne, Richard Passingham, Alvin Plough, Ronald C. Read, William Simon, Mel Stover, Edwin Tabor and Jack Yates.

I thank all the foregoing for providing me, either through the written page or by word of mouth, with suggestions and information to which I have been stimulated to add my own original touches, and hence to adapt them to the unique style and format required by this book.

Contents

Preface   6
Acknowledgments   7
Magic Starter   12
Smoke from Your Fingertips   14
Merely a Match   15
Slice the Ice   16
Find the Lady   17
Put Your Dollar on the Line!   19
The Pendulum Swings   20
Up the Mystic Number Trail   21
Ping! Things Are Not What They Seem!   22
Coins Stand Fast   23
Hopscotch Hocus   24
Z-Ray   27
Whimsical Wands   28
"Dance Ballerina, Dance"   30
Sawing a Harem in Half   32
Low and Dry   33
Unpoppable Balloons   34
Psycho Sentence About-Face   35
By Invisible Mail   36
Topsy-Turvy Dollar Bill   38
Countdown!   40
Pencil-Thru   42
Spirits in Bottles   44
Knots and No Knots   46
Personality Test   47

Checker-Cut 48
The Lady Vanishes 50
Magical Shopping 52
Match March 54
Eureka! 55
Try-Angle 56
Twister 58
Loops and Surprises 60
Penny on a Tightrope 62
Rainbow Wheel 63
The ZIG-ZAG Lady 64
Sugar Sorcery 67
Treasure Trail 68
Crazy Counting Caper 70
Match-ic 72
Brrrr!!! 73
A Series of Spells 74
Numbers, Numbers, Numbers 77
Turnabout Arrow 78
Penny Drop? 79
The Reader Escapes 80
Lucky Charms 82
Money Clock 84
A Tangled Tale 86
Snap! 88
A Three-Sided Problem 89
Clipped 90
Bewitched, Bottled and Bewildered 92
Humpty Dumpty Tumbles Again! 94
There's Magic in the Air—and in Your Hair! 95
Are you Psychic? 96
Togetherness 98
Birthday Match-Mates 99

Levitation   100
Tricky Tension Test   102
Salamander   103
Tantalizing Tangrams   104
Flower Fantastic   106
Suspended Rice   109
Marriage Lines   110
Magic Propeller   112
Topsy-Turvy Tumbler Teaser   113
Elusive Currency   114
Puzzle Magic   115
Exchequer   116
The Squeeze Inn   118
Magi-Climaxes   120
A Cure for Insomnia   125
Trickery with Words   127–128

"And now for my first trick..."

Magic Starter

There's magic right at the start and you will find it in the title of this book! Here's a trick to prove it.

1. Take a deck of fifty-two cards. (This is a full deck from which you have removed the jokers).

2. Now remove the following cards: Red aces, red twos, red threes, red fours and red fives; the black sixes, black sevens, black eights, black nines and black tens. You will have twenty cards in all. Put the remainder of the deck in a separate pile.

3. Shuffle your pack of twenty cards and place it face-down on the table. Look at the top card and show it to your friends if you have an audience. If you are trying the trick for the first time by yourself, write down the number, suit and color of your card. This is your chosen card. It is very special.

4. Place on top of your pack of twenty the cards you put aside in step two. (Your chosen card is now buried deep in the pack.)

5. Take up the whole pack at this point and deal twice as many cards from the top of the pile as there are spots (*number value*) on your chosen card. For example, if your chosen card is a red ace, (number value or spot = 1) deal two cards. If the card you selected was the black nine, deal eighteen cards.

6. After dealing the right number of cards, place the cards in your hand *face-up* upon the pack on the table.

7. Take up the whole pack again. This time, the number of cards you deal from the deck will depend on the *suit* of your chosen card. If it was a heart or a spade, deal twenty-two cards. If it was a diamond or club, deal twenty-five cards.

8. After dealing out these cards, place the cards left in your hand face down on top of the dealt cards on the table.

You will notice that all this turning over and dealing is mixing the cards thoroughly and some will now be face-up and others face-down.

9. The next deal from the deck will depend on the *color* of your chosen card. If it is a black card, deal sixteen cards. If it is a red card, deal eleven cards.

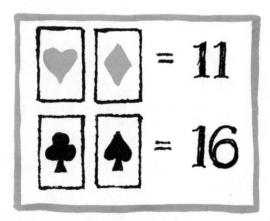

10. Again, after the deal, place the cards left in your hand face-up on top of the dealt cards on the table. Your chosen card **is** now certainly well mixed up in the pack. No one would doubt this after seeing the shuffling, dealing and turning you've been doing to the deck.

11. However, remember that I said there is magic in the title of this book. And so there is. Deal the number of letters in the title. Spell it out now as you go: JOHN FISHER'S MAGIC BOOK. Now, take a brave look at the last card you dealt on the table. There it is, your chosen card!

Smoke from Your Fingertips

For this bit of "smoke appearance" magic, you will need an ordinary safety-match box. Loosen the rough, brown, sandpaper-like material from the sides of the box. (You may have to start this process with a knife. From then on, you can probably peel it off with your fingernail.) Put the material into a saucer and light it. After it has burned itself out and cooled, throw away the loose ashes. Then wipe off the stains left in the saucer with your thumb and forefinger.

Now, you have only to rub your finger and thumb together briskly to prove there couldn't possibly be any truth to the old saying, "Where there's smoke, there's fire!"

Merely a Match

Even Paul Bunyon—for all his giant strength—couldn't have done this next trick, and neither can you. You will find that you have more than met your match in an ordinary safety match. Try it and see.

Place the match across the back of your middle finger near the tip and under your first and third finger near the top joints. Either hand may be used. Now try to break the match by pressing upward with the middle finger or downward with the other two. Try using both pressures at the same time. Do not let the thumb or little finger be tempted to help.

Give up?

Slice the Ice

Would you like to prove that you can cut through an object without dividing or separating it? If you have strength and patience you can. Here is how to do it.

Gather together the following props: a bottle (an empty ketchup bottle will do); a nine-inch length of thin, strong wire; two pencils; and an ice cube.

Twist and fasten one end of the wire to one of the pencils and twist the wire around the pencil a few times. Then fasten the other end of the wire to the second pencil in the same way. You will now have a wire firmly attached to two strong handles that will be comfortable to hold.

Balance the ice cube on the mouth of the bottle and lay the wire across the top of the cube. Pull down on the pencil handles, bearing down as firmly as you can. Very gradually the wire will cut through the cube. (This will take two to five minutes depending on pressure and room temperature.)

Finally, the wire will hit the top of the glass bottle. Let the wire and the pencils dangle over the top. Now, try to separate the two pieces of the ice cube. You sliced it in half, but it is still as whole as it was in the beginning!

Find the Lady

"Find the Lady" is the name of a card trick that has been used for ages by entertainers. It has also made money for card sharks, fooling many an unwary bettor. No one ever finds the Lady. And neither will you unless you peek—which isn't cricket.

The illustration shows the back of five cards. The Queen of Diamonds—the Lady—is in the center spot. You have my guarantee this is true. The Queen is the card marked "X."

All you have to do is place a paper clip on that spot marked X. You have clipped the Queen. Now turn the page.

Fooled again! The wily Lady wins. If you don't believe me, check it with real cards. And remember, you can't catch a Queen with a paper clip.

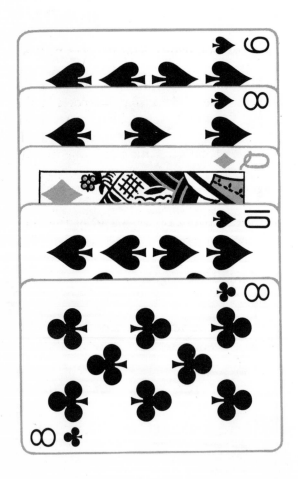

Put Your Dollar on the Line!

There's a bit of fortune-teller in every magician and I, too, have my share of this talent. But in case you don't believe me, here's your chance to stump the magician. All you need is a dollar bill and four blank sheets of paper the same size as the bill. Then follow these directions carefully:

1. Arrange the four slips of paper and the dollar bill in a row in any order you wish.

2. Note where you put the dollar bill. You may count from either left or right. Is it first, second, third, fourth or fifth?

3. Now move the dollar the same number of times as its position in the row. For example, if the dollar is second in the line, move it two times. By "move" I mean changing the position of the dollar with a slip of paper on either side of it. If the dollar arrives at the end of the line you can move in only one direction.

4. Move the dollar again.

5. And again, another move with the dollar.

6. Now, discard the slips of paper on each end of the row. You may tear them into shreds or burn them to ashes. My fortune-teller's talent tells me the dollar is not one of them.

7. Make another move with the dollar.

8. Tear, burn or throw away the slip of paper on the far left of your row.

9. Move again and discard the left-hand slip once more. Only your dollar remains. Yes?

The Pendulum Swings

When you have an optical illusion you are, in fact, "seeing things." It is as if you were to see a man walking in two directions at once. "Impossible!" you say. Of course, but not in the world of optical illusions.

Here's a fascinating way to make your eyes play tricks on you. Make a pendulum by tying a small weighted object to the end of a string about two feet long.

Ask a friend to stand across the room and swing the pendulum back and forth, back and forth.

Keep both eyes *wide* open and hold a pair of dark sunglasses over your right eye only. Now look at the pendulum.

You know it's swinging back and forth, but your eyes tell you it's swinging in a clockwise circle.

Here comes an even greater surprise. Still keeping both eyes wide open, take the dark glass from your right eye and place it in front of your left eye. The pendulum will automatically seem to change its rotation and swing in a counterclockwise direction!

Welcome to the world of optical illusions.

Up the Mystic Number Trail

Here are some mysterious number stepping stones that can take you on a fun trip. Ask a friend to help you read the numbers below from the bottom up. Each time he says a number, you say the next higher one. For example, when he says seventy-seven, you say seventy-eight. Write down the numbers you have said as you go along.

When your journey is over, turn to Magi-Climax 1 on page 120.

Ping! Things Are Not What They Seem!

Can a match pass right through one side of a closed safety pin without splitting, breaking or even meeting resistance? Can the rules governing the behavior of material things be suspended by your magic? Of course, for things are not always as they seem to be.

All you need for this trick is a kitchen match, a darning needle, a knife and a medium-size safety pin.

Cut off the striking head of the match. Then find the center of this beheaded piece of timber and make a hole at that point with the darning needle. Be careful or you'll split the match. The best way to proceed is first to make a tiny hole and then gradually enlarge it.

Stick the safety pin through the hole and close the pin. Now hold the pin in your left hand between your thumb and forefinger. (Be sure you're holding the small or curled end of the pin.)

Press down smartly and quickly at point A. The wood will seem to pass straight through the left side of the pin. It happens so fast, it will bamboozle even your most skeptical audiences.

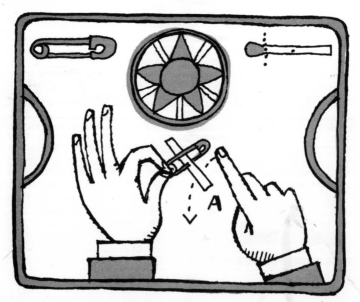

Coins Stand Fast

Two glass tumblers of the same height are needed for this neat piece of instant juggling. They should both have thick rims.

Cut a strip of smooth paper about seven or eight inches long and an inch wide. Place this strip between the two tumblers and then lay a penny at each end of the paper where it touches the rims of the glasses. The illustration will show you the setup.

It is now possible for a juggler like you to remove the paper strip without changing the position of the coins. All you have to do is moisten your right forefinger slightly and then, with finger extended, strike the strip of paper smartly across its center with a forceful blow in the direction of the arrow. Please do not hesitate. This is no time to be shy! Go ahead boldly and bring your finger down as if you were going to carry the blow right through the floor. The strip of paper will be whipped away, leaving the coins still balanced on the edges of the glasses.

Hopscotch Hocus

Three magic ingredients go into working this trick. You need playing cards set up in the magical arrangement shown on the opposite page. You will also want a small lucky charm or mascot. If you have a little china cat or dog, this will do fine. For myself, I always use a little black porcelain cat whom I call "Jinx." Your own lucky charm will do as well. The third thing you need is my magic hopping formula.

To begin your hops, concentrate on one of the red cards and place your mascot on it. You have a free choice of the red card.

Now put your magic hopper through the hopscotch moves I have outlined below and I predict you will end up on the middle card—that important and mysterious Ace of Spades. Try it and see. Remember: By a "hop" I mean transferring the charm to an adjacent card, above, below, or on either side, but *not* diagonally. Otherwise, make all your "hops" at complete random.

1. Take away the Queen.
2. Hop four times and take away the five.
3. Hop seven times and take away the six.
4. Hop three times and take away the seven.
5. Hop once and take away the two.
6. Hop twice and take away the Jack.
7. Hop five times and take away the four.
8. Hop three times and take away the nine.

How about it? Isn't your charm now resting on that majestic Ace of Spades?

Now try it again. Again, arrange the nine cards in exactly the same way. This time, though, concentrate on one of the black cards and place your mascot on it.

I predict that if you move according to the directions I give you, you will again end on the Ace of Spades. Your moves can again go any direction except diagonally. Here is the order for hopping.

1. Take away the two.
2. Hop seven times and take away the four.
3. Hop four times and take away the five.
4. Hop six times and take away the seven.
5. Hop five times and take away the Jack.
6. Hop twice and take away the nine.
7. Hop once and take away the Queen.
8. Hop seven times and take away the six.

Now do you believe that you have a lucky charm and that I have a magical arrangement and a mysterious formula?

Z-Ray

It's mysterious and uncanny. It's also true. There is a magic hole in your hand and you can see right through it! Actually there is a scientific explanation to the next bit of wizardry. So you can enjoy the trick as magic or turn on your mind and try to find the scientific twist.

All you need to see this wonder is a piece of ordinary writing or typing paper. Roll it into a tube about one inch in diameter and fasten it with a rubber band to keep it in place. You now have a magic telescope.

Hold one end of the telescope up to your right eye with your right hand. Now hold up your left hand, palm toward you, little finger touching the telescope at a point about four inches from your face.

Look through the tube with your right eye and concentrate on your left hand with your left eye. A hole has now mysteriously appeared in your left hand! And to make things more impressive, you can see objects in the room through this hole!

Cut a picture from a magazine and paste it on a piece of cardboard. Tape the cardboard to the palm of your left hand. Again, hold up your left hand, little finger touching the magic telescope. Look through the telescope with your right eye. Focus your left eye on the picture taped to your palm.

Now you can see through both the picture and your hand!

Whimsical Wands

No magical entertainment is complete without a magic wand. Here is a trick that goes way beyond that—it uses thirteen magic wands!

Look at the illustration on the opposite page and count the magic wands. There are thirteen in all. Six of the wands are spotted. Seven are plain. Now for some swift-change magic!

Trace this design on a piece of paper. You may want to paint the spotted and plain wands in contrasting colors for added effect. When your own copy is complete, check again to make sure that there are six spotted and seven plain wands.

Now, carefully cut your design into three pieces using as your guides the thin lines that divide the design into sections A, B and C. Then put the three pieces back together face-up into a rectangle. Keep C at the bottom but have A and B change places.

Count to see how many wands are plain and how many are spotted. You will be shocked and mystified to notice that these really ARE magic wands. One has changed itself! You now have seven spotted wands and six that are plain. Explain *that* if you don't believe in magic wands or that thirteen is a lucky— or unlucky—number!

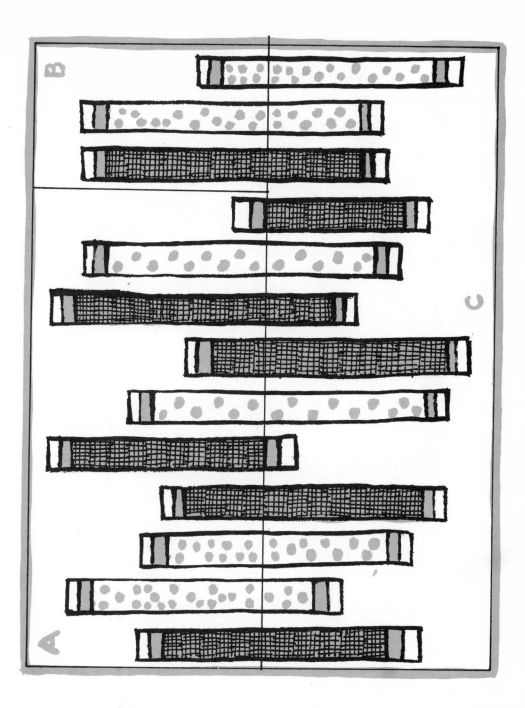

"Dance Ballerina, Dance"

Have you ever seen a handkerchief dance? You can turn an ordinary handkerchief into a twirling ballerina. And you can be the magic man to put her through her paces. It's an impressive trick to add to those you can bring out of your hat.

You will need a large handkerchief. First tie a single knot in the center of one edge as shown in Figure 2. Please notice that you do not tie the knot in one of the corners. You can still see corners X and Y left free.

Now hold the handkerchief up by the two opposite corners as seen in Figure 3. Twirl it over and over again in the direction shown in Figure 3. Twist it as tightly and as many times as you can. The more twists made at this stage, the livelier the dancing will be!

Double the twisted portion over onto itself. Hold the two ends of this part together in your right hand. (These two ends are the ballerina's feet.) Hold the single knot—which is her head—in your left hand.

Now let go of one of the feet and pull on the other. The dancer will pirouette (twirl dance) merrily on one leg. Then change your hold to the other foot and pull on the opposite leg. There she goes, whirling around again. The more you twisted in the beginning, the better the dancing will be!

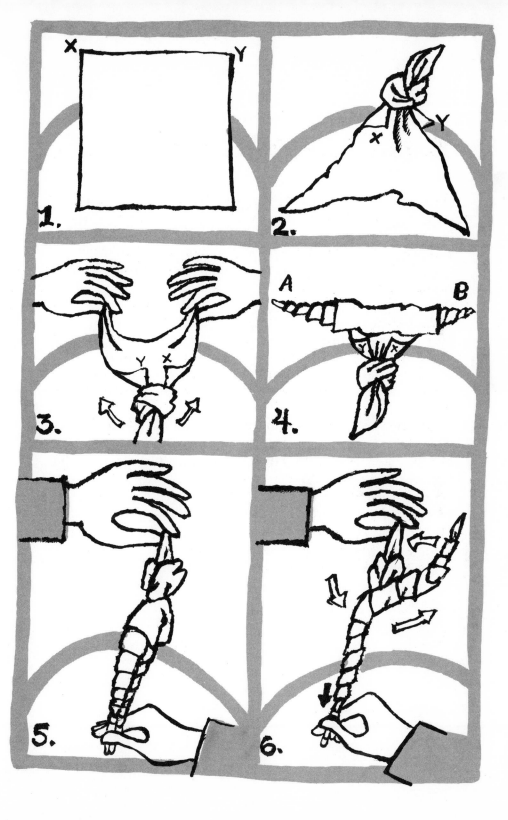

1.

2.

3.

4.

5.

6.

X   Y

X   Y

A   B

Sawing a Harem in Half

Long ago, an Arabian sheik willed his harem of seventeen beautiful girls to his three best friends. His will stated that the friend he had known longest was to receive half his harem; the next friend was to receive one-third and his newest friend was to get one-ninth.

However, when the three came to divide the seventeen girls, they found themselves in trouble. It seemed impossible to divide the girls according to their friend's wishes without getting a magician to saw one or more of them into parts. One-half of seventeen, for example, is eight and one-half. The other fractions are even more complicated, as you will see if you try to figure them out.

It so happened, however, that a great Western wizard was traveling through the land at that time accompanied by his wife. The three friends decided to ask for his advice, stating that "sawing in half" was absolutely out of the question.

This is how the wizard solved the dilemma. He appointed his wife "temporary member" of the harem, bringing the number to eighteen in all. The oldest friend then took his one-half share—or NINE Arabian ladies. The next friend took his one-third share—or SIX. Finally, the last friend took one-ninth—or TWO girls.

When all SEVENTEEN members (NINE and SIX and TWO) of the original harem had been chosen, the magician took his own wife by the arm and left. He had solved the problem and without a saw had mysteriously and mathematically "sawn" several girls, not only in halves but in thirds and in ninths. Yet they were all still beautifully whole. Never again did he come nearer to performing the absolutely impossible!

Low and Dry

Can you pick up a penny from a pan of water without getting your hand wet? It sounds impossible, but it can be done.

You'll need a shallow pan or soup plate, a penny, a quarter, two safety matches, a small tumbler or wine glass and a supply of water. Here is the magical solution!

Place the penny in the plate toward one side and pour just enough water into the plate so that the penny is completely covered. Bend, but do not break, one of the safety matches. Then, using the quarter as a weight, place it near the opposite edge of the pan with the striking end pointing out of the water.

Now act fast! Have your tumbler or wine glass all set. With your extra match, quickly light the match in the pan and IMMEDIATELY place the tumbler or wine glass in the soup plate or pan right over the top of the burning match. If you have been fast enough, water will be mysteriously drawn up into the glass, leaving the penny "Low and Dry" as I promised in the title!

Here, again, there IS a scientific explanation, and you have my permission to find it. Most of your friends, though, will be more impressed with the trick if you highlight and dramatize it as pure magic!

Unpoppable Balloons

Here is a startling trick. It startles the eyes when it works (and the ears when it doesn't). It also adds a dash of color to your collection of magical stunts.

All you will need is a few balloons, a roll of Scotch tape, a pair of scissors and several long pins with brightly colored heads.

Blow up a balloon to a reasonable size—not too big, not too small. Tie a knot in the neck. If you were to stick a pin straight into this balloon, it would surely pop with a bang. (Try it and see, if you have extra balloons you don't mind wasting.)

Now blow up another balloon, tie a knot in the neck and stick a piece of Scotch tape about an inch square on the surface of the balloon. Smooth it down gently, making sure it doesn't wrinkle. Now stick a pin through the center of the tape. Amazingly, the balloon does not pop. You can use many pieces of tape and many pins on the same balloon. Still it will not pop.

If you stick the pieces of tape on secretly and, after demonstrating what happens to an ordinary balloon when it's stuck with a pin, stick your "magic" balloon with a pin, your friends and family are sure to be amazed. Be casual about it. But be sure to stick the pins where you've put the tape!

Psycho Sentence About-Face

Here's a quick one that has a surprise ending. All you need to have on hand is a scrap of paper and a pencil. Then follow these instructions step by step:

1. Say *a* aloud. Turn to page 37 and take a quick glance at the design of words printed there in heavy letters. IMMEDI-ATELY select a creature from the upper left-hand section and say it out loud. Write down the *a* and the name of the creature you selected to go with it.

2. Say *a* again, look over the page, select a word—either "Atlas" or "Plan." Say this aloud and write the two words—*a* and your chosen word.

3. Once more, look over the page quickly. This time, settle on a geographical term from the lower left-hand section. Write it down and again place an indefinite article before it.

4. Finally, take one last look at the design and select the name of a town in South America from the lower right-hand section. Write this down.

5. You will now have a phrase combination of seven words. Repeat this three times. Then turn to Magi-Climax 2 on page 120.

By Invisible Mail

Have you ever wondered how you would get in touch with the invisible man? By invisible mail, of course, with the help of an invisible postage stamp. "But how," you ask, "can I make such an invisible stamp?" Please read on.

Place a postage stamp face-up on the table. Then fill a glass tumbler approximately two-thirds full of water. Now place a saucer on top of the glass. Set the glass-and-saucer combination directly over the stamp. Close your eyes, count to three and then open your eyes.

If you have placed the glass straight over the stamp so that none of the stamp sticks out from underneath the glass, the stamp will now be absolutely invisible!

You may walk around the glass or look down through the sides from all angles, and yet you will not see the stamp! It has completely disappeared—until you remove the saucer or lift up the glass.

It's unbelievable, incredible and invisible! Well, sort of . . .

FELLOW
FEMALE
MAN.

ATLAS
PLAN

CANAL
IZTHMUS

PANAMA
TRINIDAD
Sao Paulo

Topsy-Turvy Dollar Bill

In this trick you'll see a dollar bill turn *itself* over right in your own hands. Your friends will not believe it can really happen, but once again they will learn that it doesn't pay to challenge a magician.

1. Hold a dollar bill, George Washington side up, in your left hand as shown.

2. Fold it down the center, the long way, so George's face is no longer visible.

3. Fold the right-hand side of the bill *back*, behind the left-hand side.

4. Fold the right-hand side forward in *front* of the left-hand side. (Check the illustration to make sure you're doing it the right way.) Now, pause and take a deep breath.

5. Unfold the bill just as if you were turning the pages of a book. When you reach the position shown in Figure 6 . . .

6. . . . fold the front top edge down toward you, and the dollar bill will be upside down (even though you yourself did not at any stage actually reverse it). See what I mean?

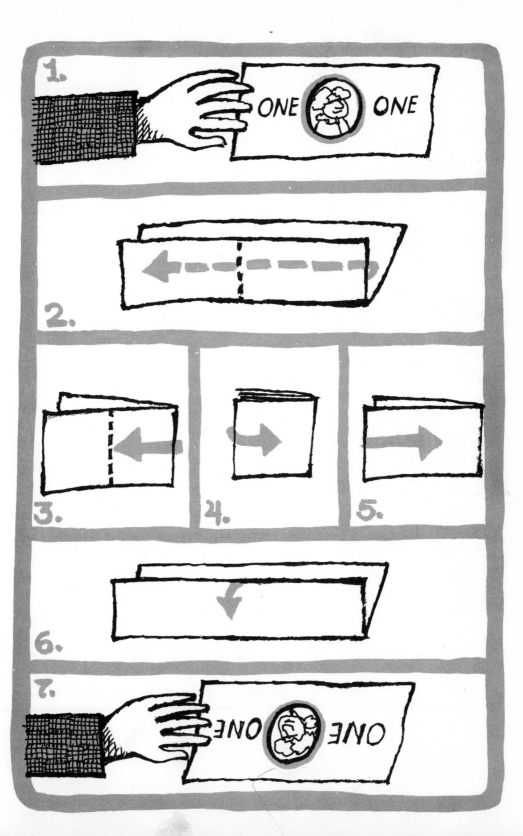

Countdown

Ten, nine, eight, seven, six, five, four, three, two, one—countdown! Here is a card trick that uses the rocket countdown to give you a startling climax. It's amazing!

For this trick you need a pack of fifty-two cards—no jokers, please.

1. Shuffle the deck. Cut it (divide the deck in half) and complete the cut (place the second half on top of the first half).

2. Deal out eight cards face-down in a pile on the table.

3. Choose any one of these. Note your choice on a slip of paper and show it to your friends.

4. Place it face-down on top of the other seven cards.

5. Then place the rest of the pack on top of the smaller pack.

6. Now, counting down as in launching a rocket, count out ten cards, laying them out face-up. But wait! You must watch out for something. When, in this backward counting, the card you deal out matches the number of your count, stop there and consider that pile complete. For example, counting backward from ten, if you get to "seven" and the card you turn up is a seven, that completes that pile. Leave it on the table face-up.

7. Continue this process for four piles, always counting down from ten. In some piles you may get through the whole backward count from ten to one without having found a card that matches. In these cases, lay the ten cards on the table in a face-up pile and cover the pile with one face-down—or blocking—card from the deck you hold in your hand.

8. When you have counted out four such piles, one of these two endings is possible:
   a. If in all four piles you counted down to "one" without finding a card that matched, you simply turn over the next card you have in the deck in your hand. IT IS THE MYSTERY CARD. It is the very card you selected in step 3.

40

b. If, in one or more of the piles, you came upon a card
that matched the number you were saying at that point
in your countdown, you are now looking at one or more
cards that are face-up. Add the number values of these
face-up cards. (If there was only one such card, use that
as your total.) If there are two such face-up cards, add
them up for your total. Now count out a number of
cards equal to your total. (This time you can count
frontwards if you wish.) Look at the NEXT card in the
deck. IT IS YOUR MYSTERY CARD!

Pencil-Thru

If you were surprised at your lack of strength earlier in this book when you couldn't break a match, you will certainly be amazed at how much more powerful you have since grown when you try the following:

From ancient times, the Chinese have had a trick in which they cut a chopstick into two halves with nothing sharper than the edge of a piece of paper. Unless you have a chopstick available, I suggest you get a pencil (it must be a full-length one) and a dollar bill.

Fold the dollar lengthwise down its center, creasing the fold sharply with your fingernail. Ask a friend to hold the pencil very tightly by the ends, as shown in Figure 1, with his thumbs on top and his fingers underneath. You yourself hold the dollar at one end between your thumb and middle finger.

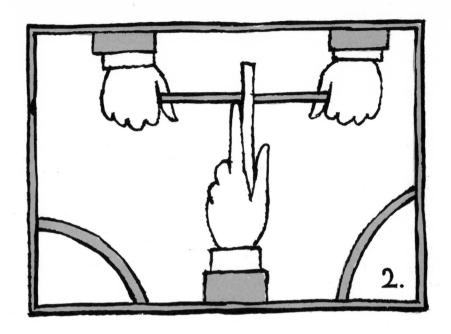

Figure 2 should make this clear. YOUR forefinger must be free to extend behind the dollar bill.

Make sure that your friend has braced himself so that the pencil will not fall from his fingers or give way when you hit down on it. Strike the middle of the pencil with the bill once, twice and then a third time. On this third time, however, you bring the dollar down with as much force as possible, and, at the same time, extend that free forefinger so that the finger strikes the pencil, too. The pencil will automatically break into two pieces if you are not afraid to strike hard with your finger and if you make sure that you follow the blow through. If your downward strike is sharp and strong and hits squarely at the middle of the pencil, you will hardly feel a thing, but the pencil will crumble as if it were made of cheese!

Long, long ago, many Chinese magicians puzzled their audiences when the chopsticks gave way. As a magician, I have a feeling that you will be equally impressed when the seemingly impossible happens! Yes, there is a trick to it. But what is magic anyway?

Spirits in Bottles

There are two good words that describe what follows—UN-CANNY and SPOOKY. This harmless exercise in a kind of spiritualism may give you an interesting and thrilling case of the CREEPS. Here's how to bring about this mysterious key dance.

Gather together four transparent glass bottles—each preferably a different size. Vinegar, salad oil, catsup and soda bottles will do. Find corks to fit each bottle. Then label each bottle with the name of a popular soft drink. You will also need four small weights—keys, screws or nails would be good. The weights must be small enough to pass through the necks of the bottles. Beside these things, you'll want some thread, a light table such as a card table, four chairs and three friends or three members of your family.

Tie each of the weights to a length of thread. Each thread must be of a different length. Then let the weights or keys hang inside each bottle and hold the threads in place by corking the bottles.

Now set the four chairs around the table and place all four bottles in an evenly spaced row diagonally across the table. Once all your props are in place, sit down with your three friends or family members around the table.

When the weights are hanging still, rest your hands, palms downward, on the table top as shown from above in the second illustration. Please remember that the keys or weights in the bottles are now completely separated and sealed from all human activity.

Somebody now calls out the name of one of the four drinks. Say, for example, someone says "root beer." Everyone now concentrates hard on the bottle you have labeled root beer. Within a short time the key inside the bottle will actually start to swing until it really goes quite wild, dashing and knocking itself against the sides of the bottle! All the other keys remain still.

While the root beer key is swinging, someone may then call out one of the other four drinks. Everyone now concentrates, let us say, on the "cider" key, and after a while the root beer key will quiet down and the cider key will begin to swing.

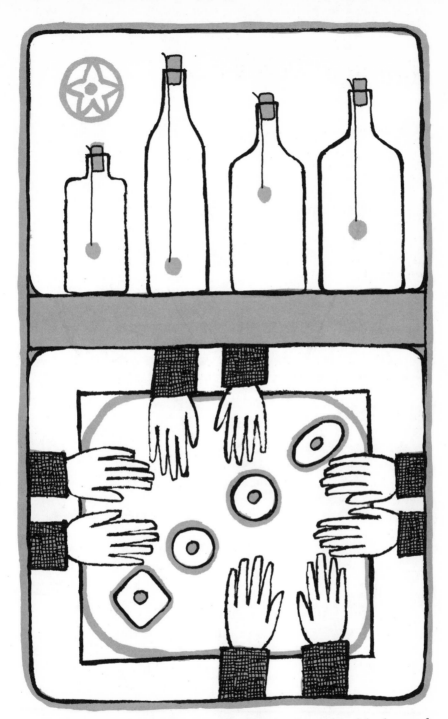

Continue until you are all finally tired out by this demanding need to concentrate, and completely baffled and mystified by this weird demonstration of spiritualism or mental telepathy—or whatever you choose to call it!

Knots and No Knots

Would you believe that a complicated bunch of knots, such as you see in the picture below, could melt away into thin air? You'll find it even harder to believe when you have carefully tied them all up yourself. For this knot-tying business, you will need sixteen or eighteen inches of soft, thick cord. Follow the directions and look at the illustrations as you do this knotting.

1. Tie a single knot in the center of the cord, right end over left. Do not pull it tight. Just keep a loose loop. *See* Figure i.

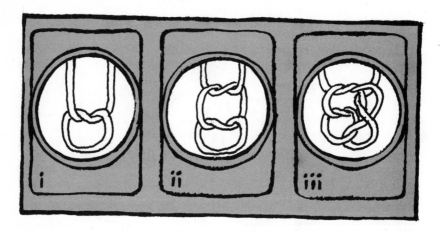

2. Now tie another single knot above this one. This time, as you tie it, place the left end over the right as shown. Do not pull it close to the first knot, but leave it in a loose loop or chain effect as you see in Figure ii.

3. The third knot is a very special one, made to strengthen the other two. Take the right end and push this through the lower loop from front to back. Then bring it from the back around to the right and in front again. Thread it this time through the second or middle loop, again from front to back. Figure iii will make this all clear.

All you have to do now is cross your fingers and slowly pull the ends of the cord taut. The knots will slide away and you'll be holding the straight piece of cord! After all that care and trouble, you'll never believe it!

Personality Test

Would you like your personality analyzed free of charge? Actually the analysis has already been done. I know that you have a five-three personality. There is really no question about it at all! If you did not have a five-three personality you would not be reading this book.

Here is a card trick that will test how correctly I have figured you out. Take any eight cards from a pack. Make sure that they are all facing the same way—either face up or down—and hold them in your left hand. Now follow these directions carefully.

1. Slide out the bottom card. Turn it over and put it back on the *bottom* of the pack.

2. Cut the cards at the center and complete the cut.

3. Place both hands and the eight cards behind your back.

4. Turn over the whole pack as many times as you wish and then stop.

5. Turn over the top two cards of the pack and put them back on top of the pack (still behind your back, of course). Then give the cards a single complete cut.

6. Keep on turning over the top two cards and follow each of these turnovers with a cut of the cards until you have no doubt at all that you have no control over the cards in your hands. That is, you do not know how many are face up and how many are face down.

7. When you feel sure of this, bring the cards back in front again and look through them. Five will be facing in one direction and three in another. This proves—without any doubt—that you ARE a five-three personality. Not a seven-one, not a six-two, not a four-four, but a FIVE-THREE.

P.S. If, as does happen once in ninety-nine times, I have misjudged your personality and one of the other combinations has resulted, please go through the trick four more times and mark down your results each time. I know that the five-three combination will, in the end, far outweigh any of the others! Now get some wise friend to tell you how GREAT it is to be a FIVE-THREE!

Checker-Cut

Amazing as it may seem, you can make a tissue paper copy of a chessboard and, after folding it several times, make a single cut to separate all the black squares from all the white squares!

First cut a square of tissue paper sixteen by sixteen inches and mark off seven lines two inches apart on all four sides. Draw in the lines. You now have sixty-four blocks, each measuring two inches square. Color every other square black.

Now fold your chessboard according to the following directions and you will get the surprising result I promised you at the start.

1. Find the center of your chessboard and fold all four corners into the center. *See* illustration.

2. Then fold AB forward along the dotted line to meet XY.

3. Fold EF across to meet CD.

4. Fold HJ forward to meet KL.

5. Fold OP across to meet MN.

6. Fold QR forward to meet ST.

7. Fold WX across to meet UV.

8. Cut through the bundle now from corner to corner along the diagonal line as shown in Illustration 8. Be careful that no squares of one color fall accidentally with squares of another. If you folded correctly, you will have an interesting result. I promise!

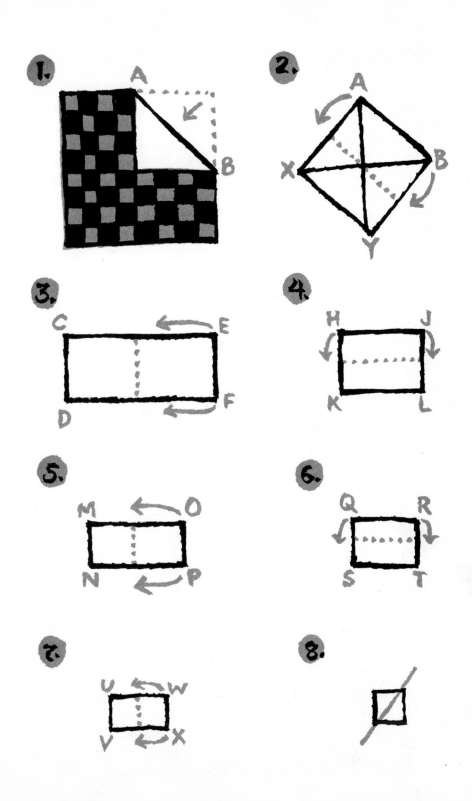

The Lady Vanishes

To make the lady in the picture on the opposite page vanish before your eyes, you need nothing but this book and your own sense of magic. But you'll want to have all the directions down pat before you start. Only then, when you know exactly what to do, will you be able to appreciate the full genius of this trick.

1. Turn your book around so that the lady is standing upright.

2. Hold the book out in front of you as far away as your arm will reach.

3. Close your left eye.

4. Stare directly at the cross to the left of the lady with your right eye. Now, this is where the magic begins to work.

5. Keep your right eye on the cross and then *slowly* move the book closer to your face.

Pop! The lady vanishes.

Magical Shopping

Once, long ago, the governments of the two neighboring countries of North Fantasia and South Fantasia decided to make it easier for magicians like you to shop in either country. They agreed that a North Fantasian dollar was to be worth exactly the same amount as the dollar of South Fantasia.

Several years passed and the government of Northern Fantasia then decreed that a South Fantasian dollar was to be worth only ninety cents in North Fantasia. To get even, the South Fantasian government ruled that from then on the North Fantasian dollar would be worth only ninety cents in South Fantasia.

Now, one of the many wizards of those magic lands happened to live in a house right on the border of the two countries and he liked to shop in both places. One day he visited a magic shop in North Fantasia, bought a new book of spells costing ten cents and paid for it with a North Fantasian dollar. For his change, he was given a South Fantasian dollar (worth ninety cents in North Fantasia).

He then crossed the border into South Fantasia, went into one of their magic shops and bought a new wand costing ten cents. He paid for it with the South Fantasian dollar and for change was given a North Fantasian dollar worth ninety cents in South Fantasia.

The wizard then went home. He still had a North Fantasian dollar just as he had had when he started. He also now had his new book of magic spells and his new wand. In addition, each shop still had an extra ten cents in its cash register. The mystery that no one has been able to solve is this: Who paid for the wand and the book? Or did the extra twenty cents appear suddenly from the land of Nowhere?

If you trace the story as it is shown in pictures on the opposite page and then cut out the map, the money, the wizard, the book and the wand, you will be able to act out the story. This will help you solve the mystery.

Put two North Fantasian dollars and two South Fantasian dollars in the cash register of both shops. Then give the wizard a North Fantasian dollar. Put the book and wand near the shops where the story tells you the wizard bought them. Now

send him on his magical shopping trip and have him buy and pay for his purchases according to the story.

As you reenact the mystery, you will find that it really does work out as the magicians of North and South Fantasia have always said. No one paid for the wand or the book, and the twenty cents earned by the shopkeepers must have been brought into being by rubbing a magic lantern!

Match March

Mothers take babies, boyfriends take girlfriends, and dog lovers take dogs for a walk. But only a magician can ever take two matches for a walk! Here's how it happens.

Take two matches from a pack of safety matches. Cut a slit or notch in the nonstriking end of one and sharpen the non-striking end of the other. Then fit both matches together to form a V as shown in the illustration. If necessary, put just the tiniest droplet of glue or paste at the point of joining to help hold the two matches together.

When this is dry, hold an ordinary table knife between your forefinger and thumb almost parallel to and about an inch from the top of the table. Place the matches over the blade at the handle end so that the top of the upside-down V is pointing ever so slightly away from you. Then lower the knife so that the striking heads just lightly touch the table top.

Now hold your hand as still as you possibly can. Then you will find that the matches, without any help from you at all, will gradually walk along the table from one end of the knife blade to the other in the most mysterious way. It is VERY interesting, and you'll find yourself doing it over and over again as you watch this silly, unbelievable march!

Eureka!

All you need for this card trick is a deck of cards and—to check your money—a pad of paper and a pencil. Take any ten cards from the deck and mix them together. When you think you've done enough mixing, think of a number from one to ten. Write it down and label it "think number." Now look at the card in your pack of ten that is equal to your think number. For instance, if your think number is seven, look at the seventh card from the top. This is your *card selection*. Write it down and show it to your audience.

Now, without changing the order of the cards in your pack of ten and still holding them face down, make the following moves:

1. Move five cards—one at a time—from the top of your pack to the bottom.

2. Say your "think number" out loud and move this number of cards (seven, for example) from the top to the bottom, one at a time.

3. Move another card from the top to the bottom.

4. Deal the next card out on the table.

5. Move the next card from the top to the bottom of the pack.

6. Deal the next card out on the table.

7. Keep on moving and dealing, moving and dealing, until you have only one card left in your hand.

Hold up the piece of paper on which you wrote your card selection so your audience can see it. Now turn the one card left in your hand over onto the table. It is your card selection! (Did you expect something else?)

Try-Angle

For centuries mathematicians and logicians have supported the idea that the whole is equal to the sum of its parts. They would say, for instance, that if you cut a pie into six pieces and then put those pieces back together again (without nibbling), you would have a whole pie.

Seems simple, yes? Seems true, yes? That's what *they* think! We magicians know better, and we can prove it by a simple example from "history."

Many years ago there was terrible flooding along the banks of the Nile River, and a small pyramid was in danger of being destroyed by the turbulent waters. So, the Egyptian Government decided to move the ancient pyramid to higher, drier ground. Here's what happened.

They cut the pyramid into big chunks according to Illustration A. Then they carried those big chunks, one by one, to the top of a nearby hill and put them back together again according to Illustration B.

Disaster! As you can see, a big hole was left in the center of the pyramid. The people of Egypt were outraged. Where was the missing piece of pyramid? They searched the area for days and nights but could find nothing. Can you figure out what happened? Remember: The height and the base of the pyramid were still exactly the same measurement as before!

(You can reenact this little-known bit of history for your audiences by tracing the pyramid in Illustration A, cutting it up along the heavy black lines and then putting it back together again according to Illustration B.)

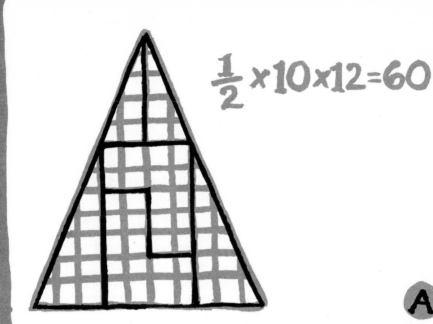

$$\frac{1}{2} \times 10 \times 12 = 60$$

A

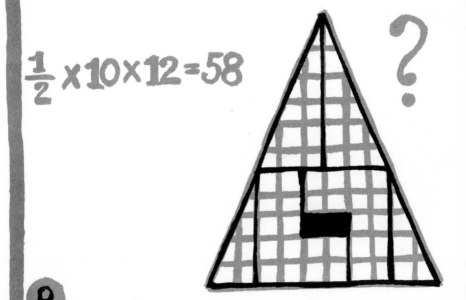

$$\frac{1}{2} \times 10 \times 12 = 58$$

?

B

Twister

Anyone would really expect that if two people followed exactly the same directions in exactly the same way, they would get exactly the same results. However, this is a book of magic, so we must be prepared for the unexpected.

For this bit of trickery you need a large, wide elastic band. Hold it as shown in Illustration A—your right thumb under and your right forefinger over the top end; your left thumb under and your left forefinger over the bottom end.

Move your right thumb forward. Move your right forefinger backward (see arrows). In this way, give the elastic band four twists, two on each side. (See Illustration B.)

Now you'll want to remove those twists (who needs twists?) by changing the position of your hands without changing your grip on the two ends. This is very easy. All you have to do is slowly lower your right hand while carefully raising your left hand. (See Illustration C.)

To reinstate the twists, as in Illustration B, merely raise your right arm while slowly lowering your left one. At this point ask a member of your audience to take the elastic band from you, putting his right thumb under and his right forefinger over the top end, and his left thumb under and left forefinger over the bottom end. He is now in exactly the same position you were in a few seconds ago, twists and all. Ask him to undo the twists, as you did, by slowly lowering his right hand while carefully raising his left.

Magic! The twists, instead of unraveling, double themselves. Now there are eight in all! And no matter what he does he will not be able to undo the twists without changing his grip.

At this point, I think it would be wise for you to take the elastic band back from him and show him how really simple it is. (He is obviously not a very good magician.)

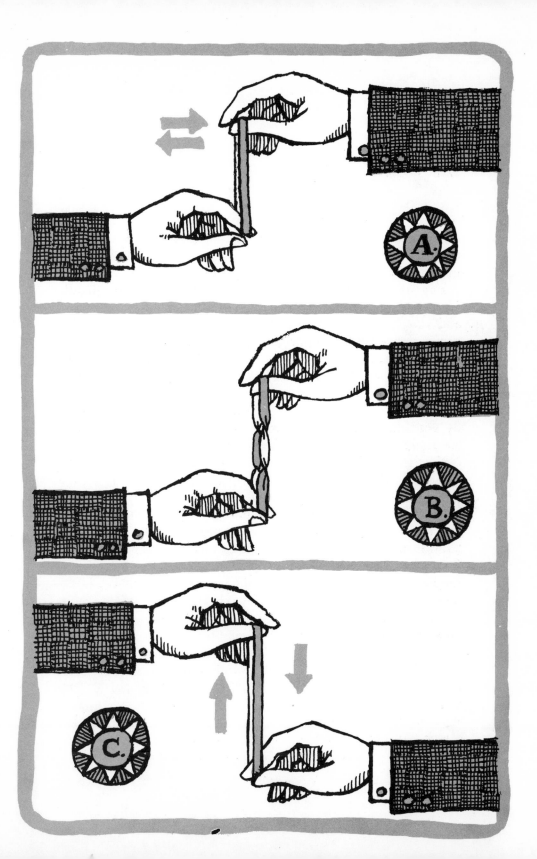

Loops and Surprises

For this very interesting exercise in tearing and looping, you'll need a bottle of glue, a pair of scissors, a ring and four strips of cloth (an old sheet is good for this). Each strip of cloth should be about three to four feet long and three inches wide. Please tear—do not cut—the old sheet into strips.

Take one of the strips and glue the ends together to form a circle or continuous loop. Make a small lengthwise cut in the middle of the cloth with a pair of scissors. Now tear all the way around the circle. You will finish with two separate loops. Of course, there's nothing particularly magical about this, but be patient.

Take the second strip of cloth and, before joining the ends together with glue, mark one end with an X. Now turn the X over so you cannot see it. You have just made a half—or 180 degree—twist in the cloth. (If you were to turn the end over again so that you would see the X, you would have made a whole—or 360 degree—twist in the cloth.)

Now glue the two ends of the cloth together so you cannot see the X. Tear all the way around this circle just as you did before. Much to the surprise of your spellbound audience, you have made one long loop instead of the two loops your audience expected.

Take a third strip of cloth. Give one of the ends a whole—or 360 degree—twist. Glue the ends together and tear around the circle. Now you have two loops, separate but linked together forever. (The tension is building in your audience. What will the great magician do next?)

Finally, take the fourth loop and slip the ring over one end. Mark that end with an X and give the strip one and a half twists—a total of 540 degrees. (First you don't see the X, then you do, then you don't.) Now glue the ends of the strip together and tear. Not only will you finish with one long loop, but that loop will have a knot tied in it and the ring will be firmly fastened to the knot. Bravo! The magician has done it again.

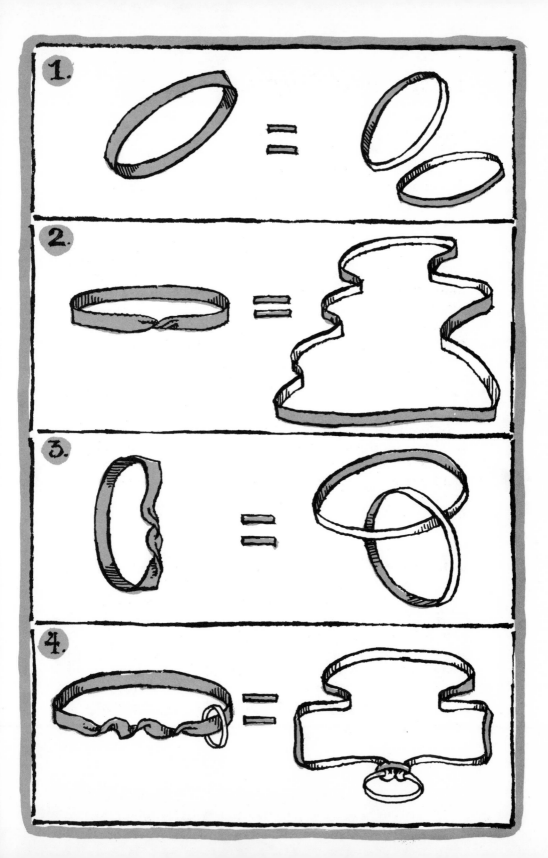

Penny on a Tightrope

Have you ever tried to balance a penny on the edge of a dollar bill? If you never have, try it now. It's not exactly magic but it's fun and it will fool your friends.

Take a fairly new dollar bill and fold it down the center lengthwise. Press your fingernail on the fold to make it as sharp as possible. (Now try to balance a penny on the sharply folded edge. It's almost as hard as trying to do it on either unfolded edge!)

Fold the dollar in half as shown in the illustration and stand it on a table top. Place a penny on the bend of the V now formed and then, with the dollar still touching the table top, gently pull the two ends of the V apart—using the forefinger and thumb of each hand. Stretch it until the dollar bill is in a straight line. Then you will see, for the very first time, a coin walk the tightrope, or at least balance neatly on it!

Rainbow Wheel

How can something be colored when it is *not* colored? Here's the answer. Copy the circle below onto a sheet of paper. Fill in the black half of the circle and the black lines with black paint, crayon or Magic Marker. Paste the circle onto a circle of cardboard the same size. Make a hole in the center and push a knitting needle through it so that you can spin the disk easily.

Now spin the disk. Mysteriously you will begin to see four complete black circles. Spin the disk still faster and the black circles will become brilliantly colored.

To make things even more surprising, spin the disk in the opposite direction. The order of the colors will be reversed!

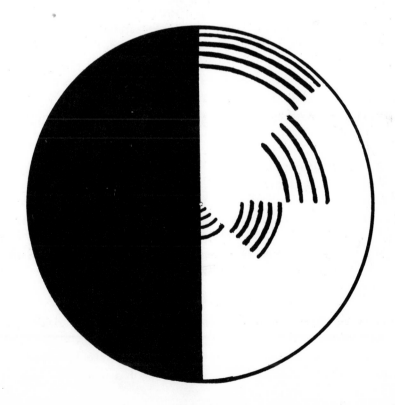

The ZIG-ZAG Lady

Have you ever heard of the great modern wizard, Robert Harbin? He says he's a "Wizard If Ever There Woz," and he is a great inventor of magical tricks. In fact, he is said to have made up hundreds of great illusion tricks.

Two of his best tricks are the ZIG-ZAG Lady (in which a girl's torso is separated from the rest of her body while she is still alive and breathing, and then moved back again) and the Electronic Cabinet (in which someone from the audience really DOES disappear!).

The trick explained below and illustrated on the following pages combines these two tricks into a fascinating paper mystery that you can do by yourself. In this, a "lady" is cut up and then made to disappear altogether.

To accomplish this you'll need a piece of strong white paper—a sheet of typing paper will do; a pencil; a ruler; a pair of scissors; and a bit of Scotch tape.

Cut the paper into a rectangle four and one-half inches wide and eight inches long. Using your ruler, measure off two-inch spaces along the long sides of the rectangle. Mark the measured spaces with dots. Draw lines across the rectangle joining these dots. Then measure off one and one-half inch spaces along the shorter sides of the rectangle and join these dots. You will now have twelve small rectangles each two inches long and one and one-half inches wide. Number them exactly as shown in Illustration A.

Then turn the paper over as if you were turning the page of a book and copy Illustration B on the other side of your paper. You may make the lady as beautiful as you wish or are able to do. Or, if drawing human figures is not your strong point, just make a stick-figure lady. The main thing is to have her head and shoulders in one space, her legs in another and her torso or middle section in the third spot. Don't forget the numbers.

Now cut along the dotted lines in the center of your rectangle. As you will see, this will make a kind of swinging door.

At this point, turn the paper over and fold this door—which is made up of the two center sections of your rectangle—back under and to the left of section six (*See* Illustration A). Fold

2	3	4	5
6	1	2	3
2	3	4	5

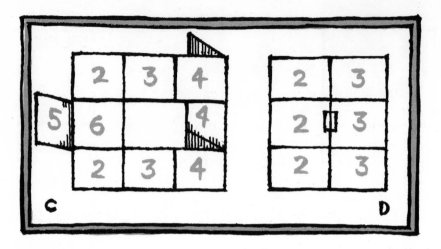

the three sections on the right—numbered 5, 3, 5,—under and toward the left. Your piece of paper will now look like illustration C, with a missing section in the center.

Your next move is to fold the three sections—numbered 4, 4, 4 in Illustration C—under and toward the left. Flip the tab marked 5 forward and to the right. You will now have a rectangle with one column of twos and another of threes facing you. Take a small piece of Scotch tape and fasten the "twos" and "threes" together (*See* Illustration D). Fold the left or "twos" column over to the right, and you will see that you have three "ones" facing you.

You now have a four-page booklet which, if you open it from left to right, will be numbered one, two, three and four. Somewhere inside is the ZIG-ZAG Lady. The problem now is to find her, for this is a most unusual book!

Turn page one and you will come to pages two and three. Then turn to page four, which forms the back cover. In order to find pages five and six—which you KNOW are there—you have to open the spine or back binding of the booklet (the edges on the right of the fourth page). When you do this, you will find pages five and six. The big mystery, however, is to find the girl herself—now, surprisingly, in one whole piece.

I will not explain how this mysterious happening takes place, but I promise that you can find her without cutting or tearing the paper in any way. Look for her carefully. She's all there, even if she has momentarily disappeared.

By the way, you will find the solution somewhere in this book, but you will have to look for that yourself! Try the Magi-climaxes!

66

Sugar Sorcery

Sugar lumps are not just for eating or for sweetening your mother's cup of coffee or tea. They can be used to show off a weird bit of number wizardry, too. For this, you'll need three cups and twelve lumps of sugar. Can you divide those twelve lumps among the three cups in such a way that there will be an odd number in each cup? All twelve lumps must be used and each must be kept whole.

There is one solution that comes to my mind, but that DOES cheat a little! You put five lumps in one cup and four in another cup. Now place the third cup so that it rests IN-SIDE the second one and put the remaining three lumps in it. Cup 1 now has five lumps; cup 3 has three and cup 2 is really holding seven lumps in all! Such cheating is, of course, not

allowed. So on we go to another solution. Pay very careful attention to the following:

1. Place the three cups in a row on the table.
2. Take one lump and place it in the cup on the left.
3. Take another lump and place it in the cup on the right.
4. And, finally, put the remaining ten lumps in the middle cup.

You now DO have an ODD number of sugar lumps in each cup! The impossible has been done again. If you do not think so, turn to Magi-Climax 4 on page 120.

Treasure Trail

You can make a deck of fifty-two cards tell an exciting tale of search for treasure. It will have all the ingredients of a great suspense story—including adventurers, lovely ladies, treasure, strong men and even a tangled love story!

The only prop you'll need for this story trick is a pack of playing cards. You won't want the whole pack, though. Use only these cards: the four aces, Kings, Queens and Jacks, and four low-value spades; four low-value hearts; four low-value diamonds; four low-value clubs.

The scene is laid on four islands. Use the aces to stand for the islands. The cast of characters includes:

Four adventurers—the four Kings

Their four wives—the four Queens

Four bodyguards—the four Jacks

The four low-value hearts will stand for love, and as you read the following story you'll see the use for the twelve other low-value cards.

This is how the story goes: There were once four islands. (Deal out the four aces face-down. All cards are to be dealt face-down in this story.) It was said that diamonds were to be had for the digging on these islands. (Deal out your low-value diamonds on top of the aces to show that there were diamonds on the islands.) Four adventurers, when they heard of the treasure, determined to go in search of it. (Deal out the four Kings on the diamonds as the adventurers.) Naturally they needed tools, so they took with them spades for digging. (Give them each a spade by dealing one of the low-value spades on each of the Kings.) When their wives heard of this dangerous expedition they decided to go along and, since they were such devoted wives, they took love for their husbands with them. (Deal out the Queens on the spades to represent the wives, and then put a low-value heart on each Queen to stand for the love she had.) As the expedition grew in size, the adventurers decided they would need bodyguards. (Place a Jack on each of the hearts. Finally, give each bodyguard a weapon by dealing out one of the low-value clubs on each Jack.)

The stage is now set. The party is on the islands. However, they have no luck finding diamonds, so the adventurers throw away their spades and desert their wives. The wives, after such rejection, tear the love from their hearts. Then the adventurers fire their bodyguards who, having no one left to guard, throw away their clubs.

At this point you step in (for this adventure obviously needs some assistance) and gather up the four stacks of cards into one pack. Then cut them as often as you like. Be sure to complete the cut each time. Now deal the cards into eight face-down piles of four cards each.

Turn each of the packs over one at a time, arranging them in lines facing you until you have all eight packs turned over and lined up. An interesting pattern has begun to appear. Can you see it? No? Don't be impatient. There's more to come.

Gather up the eight packs of cards—again in any order you wish—one on top of the other. Cut the pack and complete the cut as often as suits you. Now, deal the pack into four piles containing eight cards each.

Turn over the cards in each of the packs and spin out the fine romantic finale. The adventurers are back at work with their spades on the islands. This time they find diamonds, which they give to their wives to whom they are now reunited with love in their hearts. Each couple is again devotedly protected by the bodyguards armed with clubs. What a tale of love and treasure—and all from a deck of cards!

Crazy Counting Caper

Are you QUITE sure that you can count? You may doubt it after you've tried this crazy counting caper. All you need to do to "test" your counting ability is to trace the weird picture on the opposite page. Cut along the frame of the picture so that you have only the rectangle left.

Count the glass tumblers in the picture. Four? Right. Count them again, just to be sure. Do the same thing with the faces. There are six of them. So far, so good.

Now cut along the solid lines in the picture as indicated by the arrows. These lines separate the rectangular picture into sections A, B and C. If you now reverse the positions of sections A and B, you will find you begin to doubt your ability to count.

Count the tumblers. How many are there now? Five? Also count the faces. Five? There's crazy magic here someplace. One of the faces has been mysteriously changed into a glass. But HOW can such things BE?

Match-ic!

Here's another bit of number magic done with matches—and so the title, "Match-ic!"

1. Take five to fifteen matches from a box and lay them out in a line on the table.

2. Now lay another line of matches beneath the first. This line should contain one match less than in the first line.

3. Remove four matches from the top row and put them back in the box.

4. Count the number of matches remaining in the top row and remove that number from the second row. Put the discarded matches back in the box.

5. Remove all the matches in the top row.

6. You will now have a number of matches left on the table. Say this number out loud.

7. Now take a good look at the matchboxes below. Each contains a different number of matches.

8. Hold your right arm about twelve inches above the page, pause for three seconds and then bring your forefinger to rest on one of the boxes. Hold it there firmly for another three seconds.

9. Finally, turn to Magi-Climax 5 on page 121.

Brrrr!!!

Here is a problem that can't be solved. Or can it? You have just finished the last of that great piece of apple pie and in front of you is an empty plate and a glass of water with one lone ice cube still floating in it. You HAPPEN to have a length of string in your pocket, and all of a sudden it occurs to you to ask your family if they think you can lift that ice cube with the string without lassoing it with any knots or loops, without putting the string under the ice cube and without using your hands in the glass. Of course, they are all sure that it can't be done. The stage is set.

Since you've been leafing through this magic book, you KNOW there is a way. You really brought the whole thing up in such a casual manner because that is part of showmanship. Now your family will be suitably impressed when you, in fact, do the impossible.

Wet the string well and sprinkle salt along it on both sides. Then sprinkle salt on the cube itself. Now, lower the string and let the part you've sprinkled with salt rest on the salted ice cube while you hold the two ends in your hand. After a minute or two you will lift the cube easily, for the string will be well attached to the cube! No doubt applause will follow, and you have permission to take a bow.

A Series of Spells

Did you know that Lewis Carroll, the author of *Alice in Wonderland,* was also a talented magician and puzzle expert? Here is one of his very special card-conjuring tricks.

Before we begin, let me give you a few pointers to guide you along the way. First, the suits in this trick—spades, hearts, diamonds and clubs—make absolutely no difference. Pay no attention to them. This generous slice of wonderment has to do only with number magic. Remember, too, that throughout this trick the face cards have a special value:

King equals thirteen.

Queen equals twelve.

Jack equals eleven.

My final piece of advice is to have a large table surface for this trick and a friend around to watch you go through the complicated counting. It's easy to take the wrong route in this trick, but very exciting when you make all the right turns through Wonderland.

1. Lay out in a row an ace, two, three and four—face-up in that order. Right below these four cards, deal out a two, four, six and eight—again face-up in that order. (A two will now be directly below an ace; a four below a two, etc.)

2. On each card in the lower row, place the card whose number value is equal to the *sum* of the card in the lower row and the one above it. For example, the first card in the lower row is a two. The card above the two is an ace. So you place a three on top of the two because the *sum* of two and one (ace)

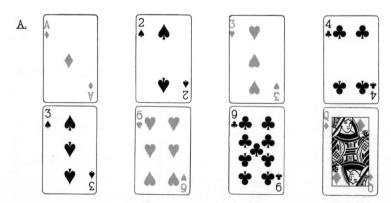

is three. Do this for all four cards and you will then have a bottom row that reads three, six, nine and Queen. (*See* Illustration A.)

Repeat this process again. The first card on the lower row is now a three. The one above it is an ace. Three and one equal four. Therefore, you put a four on top of the three spot in the lower row. When you have finished this row, you will have a four, eight, Queen and three. (*See* Illustration B.)

P.S. When the sum of the lower and upper cards exceeds thirteen, subtract thirteen from this total and use the remainder. That's how you just got three as your last card in the lower row. A Queen (or twelve) plus four equals sixteen. Sixteen minus thirteen is three. It's all very easy once you get the hang of it.

3. Continue placing cards on the lower row, as you have been doing, until you have used up all your cards. Your top row is still an ace, two, three, four. But your bottom row reads King, King, King, King.

4. Now pick up the cards in the following order turning them face down as you do so. The King pile (beneath the four), the four, the King pile (beneath the three), the three, the King pile (beneath the two), the two, the King pile (beneath the ace), the ace pile.

5. Deal out in a row the first thirteen cards face-down.

6. Deal out the next thirteen cards. But place the first card you deal on top of the second card in the row. Skip the third card. Deal to the fourth. Skip the fifth. Deal to the sixth and so on, going twice around, until you have placed the last of your thirteen cards on top of the thirteenth card in the row.

7. Pick up another thirteen cards and begin dealing. This time you will start dealing on the third card. Skip two cards. Deal to the sixth card. Skip two cards. Deal to the ninth card and so on until you place your last card on top of the thirteenth card.

8. Pick up the last thirteen cards and start dealing. This time you will deal first to the fourth card, skip three. Deal to the eighth card, skip three. Deal to the twelfth card, skip three. And so on until you have put your last card on top of the thirteenth card. You will now have thirteen packs of four cards each.

9. Pick up the thirteenth pack of cards. Place it face-down in your left hand. Pick up the twelfth pack of cards. Place it face-down on top of the thirteenth pack, which is now in your left hand. Pick up the eleventh pack. Place it face-down on top of the twelfth pack. And so on until all the cards are face-down in your left hand.

10. Now things begin to happen in this magical card kingdom. Close your eyes and spell the word *ace*. As you do, place a card face-down on the table for each letter. A-C-E. Now turn the "E" card over. It's an ace! Place this ace aside and continue dealing. This time you spell *two* out loud. T-W-O. Turn over the "O" card. It's the two! Place the two aside and continue spelling and dealing and placing cards aside right on up through the king.

11. Now pick up the pile of unseen cards that is lying on the table. Spread them out in front of you, face-up, like a giant fan. You will certainly be surprised by what you see!

Numbers, Numbers, Numbers

Magic numbers can really trip you up. But it's amusing and fun—particularly when you're baffling others. Did you know, for instance, that twelve million, three hundred and forty-five thousand, six hundred and seventy nine is a MAGIC number? Try this and you will agree that it is!

1. Write down the number on a piece of paper and then look at the arrangement of numbers below.

2. Raise your right arm, take a deep breath, count to three and then bring your outstretched right forefinger down upon one of those numbers. This is your chosen number.

3. Multiply the magic number by your chosen number and write down your answer.

4. Say your chosen number out loud nine times and then multiply the answer you got in step three by the number nine. You are now going to get a big surprise! What was your chosen number again? You've got it—over and over again.

8	1	6
3	5	7
4	9	2

Turnabout Arrow

Sometimes the simplest trick is the most impressive. Try this next one and I'm sure you'll agree.

All you need is a piece of stiff paper or cardboard, a black Magic Marker, a couple of water glasses and a supply of water.

On the card, draw an arrow about an inch long. Make it bold and dark. You want to be very sure your audience can see the way it's pointing, because at your command it will change direction.

Place the card against a wall, with the arrow pointing left. Now, put a clear glass an inch or so in front of it. The arrow still points left. Fill the glass with water and look through the glass. Magic! The arrow has changed direction.

If you would like the arrow to do another about-face, place a second glass—filled with water—several inches in front of the first. Look through this second glass and move it forward or backward until the arrow again changes direction.

Penny Drop?

Here is another of the strange things which—although they seem so easy—are really impossible to do.

Place your hands together so that palm is touching palm, finger touching finger. Then bend the middle finger of each hand so it fits between your palms. Keep the tips of the other fingers, including thumbs, together. The illustration will show you the exact position.

Then ask a friend to slip a coin in place between the tips of your two third—or ring—fingers. Now, keeping your other fingertips firmly together—not letting them separate at all—try to drop the coin. It sounds simple, but when you try it you will find, to your amazement, that your fingers are tightly locked together. In this position the coin simply CAN'T be dropped!

The Reader Escapes

Here is your chance to become an escape artist. You'll need a friend, an old jacket, a piece of cord two yards long and tied into a loop, and a lot of practice. But once you have this trick down pat, it goes zip zip zip—to the amazement of your audience.

Put on the jacket and stand up straight. Hang the loop over your right arm. Put your right hand into your right jacket pocket. Grip the material inside the pocket so the escape is that much more impossible. Let your audience examine your predicament. No tricks, no gimmicks, no gags. You can now assure everyone that you will in fact get free—without removing your hand, without taking off the jacket, without cutting or untying the cord.

Have your friend put his right hand inside your jacket. Tell him to push his hand as far down your right sleeve as possible.

With his left hand, have him push the top of the loop up the sleeve until his right hand can grasp it. Now, firmly grasping the loop, have him draw it up and out over your head.

Once the loop is safely over your head, he must then push it down your left sleeve and pull it out your cuff, over your hand, and draw it back up the other side of your arm. (Follow the arrows in the illustration.)

Now all you have to do is to let the loop drop to the floor and walk safely away—your hand still in your pocket. It's as easy as that, for a magician.

Lucky Charms

Do you have a lucky number? If you don't, it won't be long before you do. If you do, you'll soon have two.

For this charmer you'll need a sheet of paper, a pencil and a look at the long collection of charms on the opposite page. Follow these directions carefully:

1. Write down your favorite number between fifty and one hundred.

2. Look at the number on the bottom of this page and add it to the number you have just written down.

3. Add the first digit in your total to the rest of the numbers in the total. For instance, if your total is 173, add the one to the seventy-three for a grand total of seventy-four.

4. Subtract the result you obtained in step three from the number you wrote down in step one. This is your lucky number.

5. Now, starting with the charm at the top left-hand corner of the opposite page, count along the charm chain until you hit your lucky number. Remember what that charm is, and turn to Magi-Climax 6 on page 122.

Money Clock

First find twelve pennies. Then draw a clock face on a large sheet of paper and mark the hours. Follow these directions carefully:

1. Flip a coin. Did you get heads or tails? Now put the pennies down one by one, a penny for each of the twelve hours marked on the clock. *Note:* If the coin you flipped came up heads, put all of the pennies down heads-up. If it came up tails, put the pennies down tails-up.

2. Turn over the pennies at 1, 3, 4, 5, 8 and 10 o'clock.

3. Next, turn over any six coins. It doesn't matter if you turn over pennies that were turned in step two. Any six will do. You have a perfectly free choice.

4. Although I have not been able to watch what you've been doing, I will now help you divide your coins so there are an equal number of heads and tails. Watch carefully.

5. Push aside the coins at twelve and two. (Do not turn them over.)

6. Push aside the coins at eleven and six.

7. Push aside the coins at nine and seven.

Now check the coins you have taken from the clock face. I'll bet they match the ones left on the clock. For instance, if you have two heads and four tails still on the clock, you will have two heads and four tails in your "discard" pile. Right?

A Tangled Tale

I hope you have some time on your hands for this next trick because you're going to need it. But don't despair. As one magician to another, I can tell you the results are well worth the effort.

You will need a five-foot length of string which you tie into a loop. Then follow the directions very carefully, checking with the illustration as you go.

1. Hang the loop of string over your left palm as shown.

2. With your right hand, take hold of the two strands now hanging about twelve inches below your left palm. Bring the strands up behind the back of your left hand and then arrange them as shown—strand X between fingers two and three and strand Y between fingers four and five. Finally, bring both strands behind your thumb.

3. Pull the strands around your thumb and across your hand. Give the strands a half twist in the process and arrange both strands as shown. Strand Y should be between fingers four and five and strand X should be below finger five.

4. Give another half twist back across your hand and place strand X between fingers two and three and strand Y between fingers one and two.

5. Now bring Y above X and take the two strands around your thumb at point A. Then lift them over your thumb, passing both strands between fingers three and four.

6. Let your audience examine the complicated mess you've made.

7. Pull the string at point B toward you. The whole contraption will melt right through your hand!

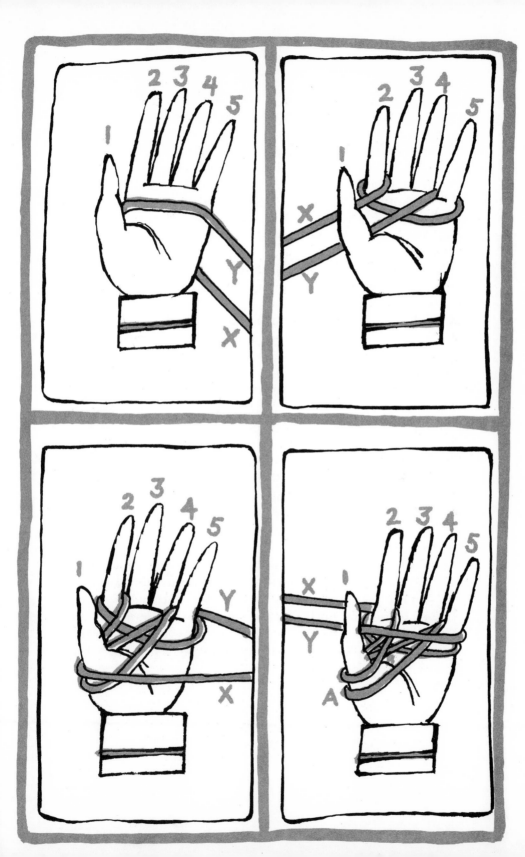

Snap!

Shuffle a full pack of fifty-two cards and then take out nine cards valued from ace to nine. The suit doesn't matter. You just need a series of nine cards—ace through nine.

Arrange these nine cards in numerical order in a *face-up* pile on the table. The ace should be at the bottom of the pile, the two should be second, and so on until you've placed the nine on the top of the pile. Now turn this pack over and hold it face-down in your left hand.

Without disturbing the order, take the top three cards and place them in a small pile on the table at your far left (A). Take the next three and place them in front of you (B). Then place the last three to your far right (C). Put pile A on top of pile B, and then place pile C on top of B and A.

At this point move the cards, one at a time, from the top of this "nine" pile to the top of the main pack. At any time you wish, STOP—and then place the card box on top of the cards left in your pile of the "nines." Whether you leave one, two or more cards in this "nine" pile depends upon you.

Now gather up the rest of the deck, shuffle it and cut it anywhere you wish into two piles. Count the cards in one of these piles. If the result of this counting is a two-digit number, add the two digits together. If, after adding, you still have a two-digit number, keep on adding the digits together until you have a single digit. Jot down this number. For example, if there are nineteen cards, one and nine total ten, and then one and zero total one.

Go through the same counting and adding process with the other pile until you have another single-digit number. Add these two numbers together. If the result is a two-digit number, keep on adding until you have a single-digit number.

Say this final number out loud three times. Go back to the small pile of cards you left underneath the box. Turn over the top card. Snap!

A Three-Sided Problem

For this trick you'll need six containers—glasses will do—and a full deck of 52 cards.

Arrange your containers as shown in the illustration and think of them as A, B, C, D, E and F.

1. From the deck, take the six cards shown below and arrange in a row as indicated.

2. Shuffle the rest of the pack and take another card. This card may be of any suit, but it must have a number value ranging from ace to seven. Place this card face-down in the row in the spot marked in the illustration with a question mark. Only *you* know the value of this mystery card.

3. Whatever the number value of the mystery card, place that number of cards into each of the containers. For example, if your mystery card is a four, place four cards in each container.

4. Now deal the rest of the cards in your hand in this way: one card to each container listed: C-B-C-D-D-F-E-B-C-B-C-E-E-C-B. Then, dealing one card at a time, C-E-B-C-E-B and so on until you have none left.

5. Your containers form a triangle. And like all proper triangles, it has three sides: ACF, ABD and DEF. Choose one of the sides. Now take the cards in the two end containers (for instance, A and F) into the middle one (C).

6. Now turn over your mystery card. Add the number value of your mystery card to the number values of six face-up cards. Say this number out loud!

Now count the cards in your chosen container. Say this number out loud! The two numbers are the same!

Clipped

Three large paper clips, a twelve-inch length of cord and a piece of fairly stiff paper are at the heart of this most amazing "stringing up" trick. The paper should be a little larger than a dollar bill—about eight inches by four inches. You could use a real dollar bill, but it is easier and cheaper to use a piece of paper.

Here are the simple directions, which you also see illustrated on the opposite page:

Fold the paper lengthwise (as shown in Figure 1) and measure it off into three equal parts.

Label them A, B and C. (If you use a dollar bill, you will have to be careful to remember the sections as A, B and C.)

Bend section A back against B, and bend C forward behind B. Crease the folds and stand the paper up in a "Z" shape as in Figure 2.

Now take one of the paper clips and push it over B and C, clipping them together (Figure 3).

Take the second clip and push it over A and B (Figure 4). You will notice that B is now clipped to both A and C.

At this point, place your loop of string or cord over B and C near the crease and in front of both paper clips (Figure 5). Now take one more paper clip and place it over A and B but not including C.

Finally, ask someone from your audience to hold the string at X. You take hold of C and A and pull them apart gently and slowly. This first pull will cause the three clips to move together. Now give a final tug. All of the clips will be forced off the paper (or bill) and will hook themselves into a chain (Figure 7). It works—and it never fails to surprise.

Note: If you do not have an audience, you can, in the last step, hold the cord at X with your teeth.

Bewitched, Bottled and Bewildered

Have you ever had a secret wish to be a detective? Well, let's see how good you are at explaining mysteries.

Here is the story of the "Vanishing Wine Bottles" or "How the Butler Got Away With It—For a Time." It's up to you, the expert, to explain why the master's plan to keep track of his wines didn't work and why he needed to call you in to solve the mystery.

To reenact the crime you will need thirty-two matches to represent the wine bottles, and a clear table top. The master felt quite certain that his stock of wines was disappearing more rapidly than he was serving them to himself and his guests. He suspected the butler. But, being a fair man, he did not want to accuse him without evidence. So he devised a plan, he thought, whereby he could keep count of the wine bottles in his cellar.

He arranged the bottles in rows. Nine across the top row. Nine across the bottom row. Nine down each side. (*See* illustration.) Each night the butler continued to steal bottles of wine. Each morning the master counted the nine bottles across the top and bottom and nine on either side.

After the third night the master realized that his stock of wine looked considerably smaller. He again counted across top, bottom and sides and found nine each way. Nevertheless, it looked all wrong, so he called in *you*, the expert, to solve the problem.

Here's how you did it:

Arrange your matches in the pattern the master ordered for the first night. Then, move "bottles" ABCD to new positions (as shown) and "steal" EFGH. Now, count. Nine across the top. Nine down each side. Nine across the bottom.

To explain the butler's activities on the second night, move "bottles" IJKL and "steal" MNOP. Count again. Nine on all four sides.

The third night, the butler moved QRST and stole UVWX. Still, the count of nine, but the master noticed a thinning of bottles on the shelves.

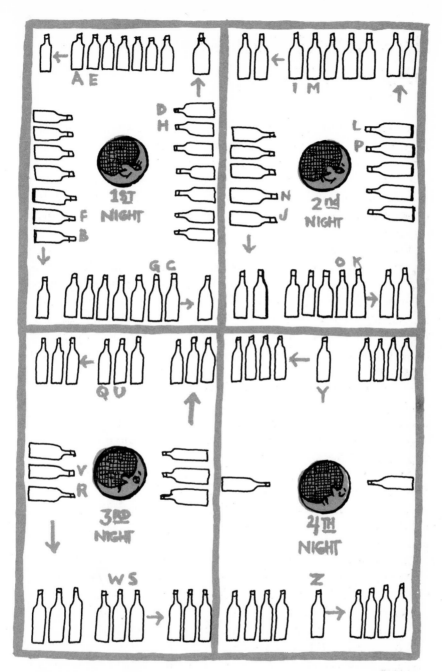

The fourth night, the butler moved Y and Z and stole the other two, leaving nine across each way. You were in on it by then, though. You watched him, caught him red-handed and were able to unravel the whole puzzle for the master.

Can your friends do the same?

Humpty Dumpty Tumbles Again!

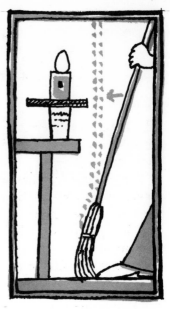

Have you ever sat spellbound while a stage or television juggler did his tricks? Well, sit no longer! Here is an instant juggling act that can be mastered with little practice. It will give you the sparkle of a real performer.

Line up a table, a glass tumbler, a hard-cooked egg (after mastering this trick, you may use a raw one), the striking cover of a *box* of kitchen matches, a shallow square tin baking pan, and a broom with stiff bristles—and lots of spring in the bristles.

Fill the glass about two-thirds with water. Place it near the edge of the table. Put the baking pan on top of the tumbler as shown. The pan should extend *out* about an inch or two over the table edge. On top of the pan, stand the striking cover of a box of matches with the egg—pointed end-up—balanced in the open end of the box.

Stand the broom up so that it touches the edge of the tray as shown by the straight dotted line in the illustration. Then place your foot on the bristles and pull the broom handle back toward you and away from the edge of the table and the tray. Count to three, take a deep breath and let go of the handle.

Your broom will spring back against the table and tray with amazing results. The tray and the matchbox will be knocked smartly away and the egg will fall into the water without breaking—and with an impressive PLOP!

Note: If it didn't quite come off the first time or two, keep at it. You'll get the hang of it. But be sure to use a hard-cooked egg while you're learning.

94

There's Magic in the Air—and in Your Hair!

This trick is rather like a scientific experiment. It calls for a steady hand, a coin, a match, a thin water glass, a comb and some hair.

Very carefully, balance the coin on its side and lay the match —ever so gently—on the edge of the coin. Carefully set the glass over this arrangement.

What you have to do now is make the match fall off the coin without:

1. Moving, lifting or touching the glass
2. Disturbing any cloth or covering that happens to be on the table
3. Touching the table
4. Stamping on the floor
5. Moving the coin in any way

And yet it is possible. Take a comb and run it briskly through your hair several times. Then hold the comb close against the glass *without moving the glass*. The match will fall mysteriously as the comb touches the glass. Can you explain why, or would you rather settle for magic?

Are You Psychic?

Some people have wonderful powers of concentration and an extra sixth sense about numbers. Maybe you are one of them. Then you must be psychic! On the opposite page is an interesting arrangement of cards. See if by concentrating on certain cards and blocking out others, you can select cards that will alternately add up to the number I have in mind.

For this experiment, get four coins—pennies, nickels or dimes. Any coins will do. You will also need ten large kitchen matches or strips of paper about the same size.

Here's all you have to do: Let your eyes wander over the arrangement of cards and, after ten seconds, make a selection. Put one of the coins on your chosen card. Now with your matches, cover all other cards in the same vertical (up and down) row and in the same horizontal (left to right) row as the card you selected.

Concentrate on the remaining nine cards. Select one and put a coin on top of it. Again, block out all other cards in the same horizontal and vertical rows as the card you selected. There will now be four cards left uncovered.

Concentrate and select one of these four cards. Put a coin on top of the card, and again, block out any cards in the horizontal or vertical rows. There is now only one card left uncovered. Put your last coin on it.

Now add up the value of the cards you have *covered with coins*. Count ace as one, Jack as eleven, Queen as twelve and King as thirteen. Keep the slip of paper on which you did the addition, and turn to Magi-Climax 7 on page 122.

Togetherness

The strange line of numbers and letters printed on this page can make sense—magically—if you use a deck of fifty-two playing cards to help you discover its meaning. You'll also want to have on hand a single die (dice) and a shaker or a small glass. Here are the steps to follow:

1. Shake the die and look at the number that turns up. Count that number of spaces from *either* right or left on the chart below. Suppose the die shows four and you choose to count from the right. Your card on the line of numbers and letters would be an ace. Write down your selection on the sheet of paper.

2. Shake the die again. Read the number that turns up. Count off spaces from the *other* direction on the chart. In other words, if you counted from right to left the first time, you will now count from left to right. Write down this selection. You now have two chosen cards.

3. As you know, seven is something of a magic number for many people. Therefore, just to be interesting, let's remove all the sevens from the deck of cards you've been holding in reserve. Lay the sevens aside for future reference.

4. Shuffle the rest of the deck thoroughly. Cut the pack and complete the cut. Do this three times to make very sure it's well-mixed.

5. Now place three of the sevens at the bottom of the deck and one on top.

6. Give the deck one more cut. Complete the cut.

7. Very carefully, turn over each card one by one. Somewhere within the deck you will find your two chosen cards sitting side by side. How's that for togetherness!

Note: This amazing trick works ninety-nine times out of a hundred. If you had the bad luck to hit that one chance, try the trick over again. It's bound to succeed the second time.

Birthday Match-Mates

There are, as you know, 365 days in a year—plus an extra day during leap year. With that in mind, if you were at a party or a club meeting attended by thirty people, how great do you think the chances are that there will be at least two persons present with the same birthday?

I predict—with almost absolute certainty—that you will always find at least one pair of birthday match-mates. Why not test out my prediction at your next meeting? Hand out slips of paper and ask each person to jot down his or her birthday. Or, if you prefer, have each one write down the birthday of a friend not present in the group. Ask them to fold the paper and hand it back to you. The only rule to follow is that no two of your subjects are to compare notes.

When you check the birthdays, you will find—with the rarest exception—that there will be at least two falling on the same date. Two birthday match-mates out of at least 365 chances!

P.S. If you don't happen to meet with a group that large, pick birthdays of famous persons by opening a book such as *Who's Who in America.* Simply take one from each of thirty pages, putting your finger on a choice quite by chance.

Levitation

To levitate means to lift in a magical manner. And in this experiment—which uses a touch of hypnotism in addition to magic—you and a few of your friends will have the fun of doing the impossible. You will lift or levitate another friend with your fingertips!

To do this you need the cooperation of four friends.

Ask the person to be levitated—the subject—to sit in a chair and relax. Now two people stand on the subject's right side and two on his left. Each of you close your fists. Hold your two hands together with your forefingers extended as shown in Figure 1.

One person places his two extended fingers under the subject's left armpit. The second person positions his extended

forefingers under the subject's right armpit. The third places his forefingers under the subject's left knee. And the fourth person puts his fingers under the subject's right knee. Now try to lift the subject. You will find that it is IMPOSSIBLE to do. That is, it is impossible without a bit of hypnotism and some levitating magic. Here's how you put that to work for you.

Again have the subject seated in a relaxed position in the chair. Now you and your lifters place your four pairs of hands on the subject's head—one hand on top of the other. Press down firmly, but not so hard as to cause pain.

Continue to press down with a steady pressure, counting aloud to ten. Then give the command for your lifters to take their hands off and quickly extend their forefingers to assume the lifting position.

Now ready, lift. Amazingly, the subject will have become so much lighter that he will go soaring several feet in the air. He has been miraculously levitated with eight fingers!

Tricky Tension Test

Do you like to take stock of your strength now and then? Here is a test you *can't* pass—and your Dad can't either!

In the middle of a five- or six-foot length of cord, tie a fairly heavy book. Take the ends of the cord in your hands and wrap each end around your fists a few times as shown in the illustration. This will give you a good, strong grip on the ends of the cord.

Now, pull with all your might and try to straighten out the cord along an ABSOLUTELY LEVEL PLANE. It seems so easy. But, strange as it seems, it can't be done! (If it looks like a level plane to you, your eyes are fooling you. Rest a large tray or cookie sheet over the stretched cord and you will see that it is not PERFECTLY straight.)

Salamander

After you have done this experiment, you will probably wonder what the title has to do with it. Be patient and you will understand.

To do this little bit of mystification, all you need is an old handkerchief (or a square of old fabric); a fairly large coin such as a quarter or a half dollar; and a punk—the kind you use on the Fourth of July to light sparklers.

Place the coin under the middle of the handkerchief and twist the fabric around it securely. Next, light your punk and have it glowing red. Now, hold the twisted ends of the handkerchief in your left hand and the glowing punk in your right. Press the lighted punk firmly against the handkerchief. Don't be afraid to burn your handkerchief. Magically, it will not burn. Unwrap the coin and look at the fabric. It may be discolored by smoke, but it will not be destroyed.

What on earth could the title, Salamander, have to do with this trick? Well, if you look up this word in the dictionary, you will find that it is defined as a little lizard-like creature *and* the name of a NONEARTHLY, nonreal animal from the land of mythology, who could endure fire without being burned. In fact, ancient peoples—who believed that there were just four elements: earth, fire, air and water—really believed that this nonreal creature lived in the element fire. Your handkerchief is your mythological salamander, for the fire of your punk didn't burn it!

Tantalizing Tangrams

The Chinese have a name for them! They call these 4,000-year-old puzzlers "Tangrams," after the legendary Chinese puzzle inventor, Tan. He is famous for taking a square of black cardboard and cutting it into seven shapes from which an endless number of charming Oriental figures could be made.

But Tan's figures were not just interesting forms or shapes. They had—and still have—a magical turn that continues to baffle and entertain. Try them and see for yourself! The only props you'll need are a piece of paper (colored makes it more interesting), a ruler, a pencil and a pair of scissors.

Begin with a square of paper. Draw the lines exactly as you see them in the illustration on this page. Then cut along the lines. You will have seven pieces—triangles, squares and rectangles. The only rule for this game is that you must use all seven pieces in each picture you create.

Before you try to re-create the pictures on the opposite page, take a look at them. Put your imagination to work and you will see in Figure i, two Chinese men. Both are made from all seven pieces, but one is missing a foot! How can this be?

In Figure ii, you can first see a mechanic's wrench, then a Japanese girl in a kimono making a bow and, third, a baby carriage. All have been made from the seven mystery pieces. Can you make them?

In Figure iii, there are two pigs but one has lost its tail. How did this happen when all seven pieces were used to make each pig? Finally, in Figure iv, the seven pieces form another square with a section missing from the corner. Can you rebuild the square losing a corner but still using all seven pieces?

When you have puzzled over these long enough, turn to Magi-Climax 8 on page 123 for the solution to these Oriental mysteries.

Flower Fantastic

Would you like to make a magic paper flower that will bloom in six different colors at the touch of your fingertips? It will take some time and patience and you will have to follow the directions step by step, watching the illustrations on the opposite page as you go along.

For this you will need a long strip of paper (shelf paper will do); crayons or paints; a pair of scissors; and some glue. Cut a strip of paper one and one-half inches wide and about eighteen inches long. This strip must be marked off into nineteen equilateral triangles. (An equilateral triangle is one having all three sides exactly the same length.)

Here's one way to do it: Measure one and three-quarter inches from one end of the *top* of the strip. Mark this place with a dot. Draw a diagonal line, one and three quarter inches long, from the dot to the bottom corner of the strip. Cut along this line. (*See* Figure 1.) Now measure one and three-quarter inches along the *bottom* of the strip and make a dot. Draw a diagonal line one and three-quarter inches long from the *top corner of the strip* to the dot you just made on the bottom of the strip.

Again measure one and three quarter inches along the *top* of the strip and make a dot. Connect this dot with the point where your diagonal line touches the *bottom* of the page. You will now have two equilateral triangles—triangles that are one and three-quarter inches on all sides.

Repeat this process until you've made nineteen triangles. Crease all the diagonal lines back and forth so they will bend easily. Number the result as shown in Figure 1.: 1-2-3-1-2-3, etc. Leave the last triangle blank.

Turn the strip over. This time leave the first triangle blank and number this side 4-4-5-5-6-6-, exactly as shown.

Color all triangles marked 1, red; all those marked 2, green; and all those marked 3, yellow. On the other side, color all those numbered 4, blue; all those numbered 5, orange; and, finally, all those number 6, purple. Leave the unnumbered triangles blank.

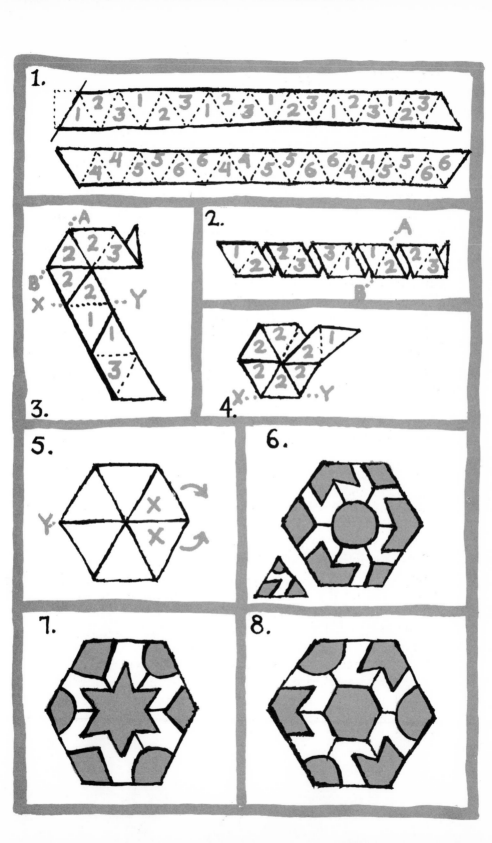

1.

2.

3.

4.

5.

6.

7.

8.

Now fold the strips so that the colors on this second side face each other: purple on purple, orange on orange, blue on blue, etc. Your result will be a shortened strip with numbers appearing as they do in Figure 2.

Fold the longer end of the strip back along the line *ab*. Your result will look like Figure 3.

Fold again along line *xy*. This will give you the pattern seen in Figure 4. There will be six green or number 2 triangles grouped together, with one triangle left over. Fold the blank side of this triangle and glue it to the corresponding blank triangle on the other side.

If you have assembled the flower correctly, you will now have six green triangles facing you. Now, let's watch this cluster bloom as a flower—first one color, then another as you manipulate the flower with your fingers.

Pinch together any two triangles (*xx* in Figure 5). Don't hold them near the line that divides the two triangles. Push down with your thumb and forefinger. At the same time, with your left hand grasp the point at which the two triangles on the opposite side meet (*y* in Figure 5). Push down and in toward the center. As you see the new color coming up, you may have to use your left hand to turn the entire blossom inside out. It will be another flower color!

Continue in this way, pinching the two triangles that come up at the *x* point and pushing down and toward the center on the tip of the two triangles opposite *y*. Each time a flower of a new color will show its face.

A time will come when it will no longer be possible to bring up a new complete flower. Then turn the flower one petal in a clockwise direction and work from the triangles that have come to the *xx* and *y* positions. It will be possible to produce different colored flowers with this grouping of paper triangles for as long as the paper holds out, if you continue to move one petal clockwise when you notice that the flower can no longer produce a full set of matched petals.

Suspended Rice

As you know, levitation means making something heavy rise into the air, which seems to hang there by magic. All magicians like to prove they can levitate a person or thing, for it is eerie and very mystifying. The Mango Trick—or the Basket Illusion —is famous all over India, where it is a specialty of street magicians. You can do it, too, if you follow these directions carefully:

Find a jar whose body is wider than its opening. A small goldfish bowl would be ideal.

Fill the jar to its brim with uncooked rice. Keep pouring in as much rice as possible. When the jar is filled, pack down the grains firmly with your hands. Take hold of a long, dull knife and plunge it straight down into the jar. Quickly withdraw it, and then plunge it down again.

Keep plunging the knife into the rice with quick jabs, each about an inch or so deep. As you make each jab into the rice, the kernels will pack more tightly around the knife.

After about ten such thrusts, *really* plunge the knife down as far as it will go. (If you placed enough grains of rice in the jar, you are about to see a very strange happening!)

Cross your fingers, imagine you are in India and then lift the knife. The jar and all the rice in it will be mysteriously lifted into midair.

Note: This trick has another benefit. After you're through you can cook the rice and eat it.

Marriage Lines

You don't have to be married to do this gymnastic trick with wedding anniversaries and birth dates. Get all the information you need from your mother or father or some of their married friends. And now get set to impress a whole gathering with your number wizardry.

1. Copy the chart shown on the opposite page.
2. Write down the husband's age in the blank provided.
3. Below it, write in his wife's age.
4. Under that, fill in the number of *whole years* this couple has been married. In other words, write down how old these people are and how long they have been married as of the last day in December, 1971.
5. Add together all three numbers and write down the total.
6. Write the magic number for 1971 (87) in the line marked X.
7. Add the two numbers for Total A.
8. Now mark down the year the wife was born.
9. Below it, write the year of the wedding.
10. Add these together to get Total B.
11. Bring down Total A and add to Total B.
12. This will give you Total C.
13. Subtract Total C from 6,000 and you will come to the surprise in this number twister.

Regardless of the fact that the husband's age has been completely muddled with that of his wife, the wedding date has been thrown in with a couple of other odd numbers, and the husband's year of birth was never introduced, the answer will be the year the husband was born!

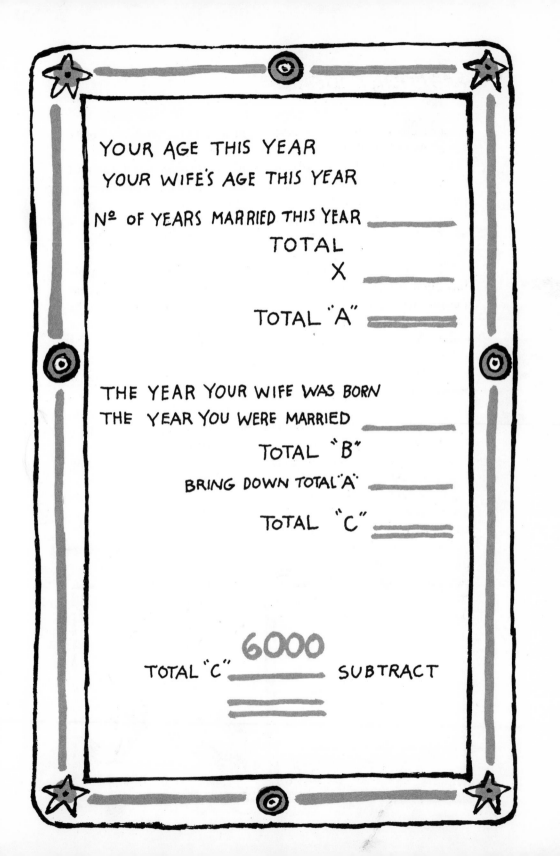

YOUR AGE THIS YEAR

YOUR WIFE'S AGE THIS YEAR

Nº OF YEARS MARRIED THIS YEAR _____

TOTAL

X _____

TOTAL "A" _____

THE YEAR YOUR WIFE WAS BORN

THE YEAR YOU WERE MARRIED _____

TOTAL "B"

BRING DOWN TOTAL "A" _____

TOTAL "C" _____

TOTAL "C" ____ 6000 ____ SUBTRACT

_____

Magic Propeller

Here is a most interesting motor that will not be much trouble to make and will be quite entertaining to you and your friends.

You need a piece of soft wood about ten inches long and about three-eighths of an inch wide and thick. Cut notches about one-eighth of an inch deep along this piece of wood. (You will need to make notches for about eight inches.) Then cut a propeller about two and a half inches long from a piece of thin tin.

Fasten your propeller to the end of the notched wood by driving a nail through the metal and then into the tip of the wood. You must make sure that the metal propeller fits loosely on the nail. Only then will the propeller spin as easily as you will want it to.

Now hold end B of the propeller shaft in your left hand and rub a pencil across the notches. The propeller will begin to revolve. The faster you rub, the faster it spins around.

The uncanny thing is that if you rub along one edge of the notches, the propeller revolves in a clockwise direction. If you then start rubbing on the other edge, and keep rubbing at about the same speed, the propeller will slow down, stop and then change its direction!

In the Orient this device is a favorite form of mystification and amusement for young children. However, you will often find experienced magicians discussing its "why and wherefore" and wondering HOW it really does work. To be truthful, I don't really know why it works myself!

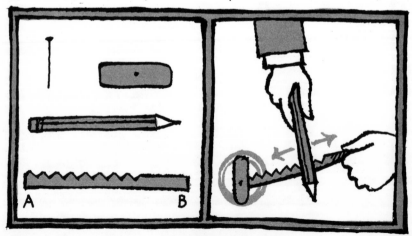

Topsy-Turvy Tumbler Teaser

Here's a good after-dinner puzzler to pose for the family. It will keep some people confused for quite a while. And, of course, when you come up with the easy solution, you'll look like the wizard you really are. Practice the moves in private many times so that you can do it fast and with a real magician's flourish.

All you need for this is three playing cards—an ace, a two and a three—and three water glasses. Present the puzzle this way:

Here are three glasses standing upside down in a row. Each is resting on a playing card—ace, two and three. From now on the number of the card is the name of the tumbler.

I will now turn over tumbler two so that it will be right side up.

The problem is this: You must turn the tumblers so that all will be right side up. However, you may have only three turns and you must turn *two tumblers at a time,* holding one in each hand.

When someone has succeeded in solving this, ask another person to try it. This time, have tumbler one and three right side up and turn tumbler two upside down. Present the puzzle again giving the same rules, except that this time all the tumblers must be turned upside down! It's mystifying, confusing and topsy-turvy!

P.S. The order for turning the tumblers that will unlock the puzzle in either case is:

    a. Turn tumbler 2 and 3
    b. Turn tumbler 1 and 3
    c. Turn tumbler 2 and 3

Elusive Currency

Don't let it elude YOU! In other words, catch it IF YOU CAN. But I'll bet you can't! Here is a challenge that seems so easy but turns out to be impossible. If you don't believe me, try it and see. You'll need a fairly new dollar bill and a friend to help you out.

Hold one end of the dollar between your finger and thumb. Ask your friend to place his own finger and thumb near each side of the bill at the center—right over George Washington's picture *but not touching it.*

Wait a minute or so. Your friend must not know exactly when you plan to let go.

All of a sudden, when he least expects it, release your hold on the dollar. The bill will slip right through his fingers! It is impossible for him to catch the dollar under these conditions! Have him hold the bill and you try to catch it if you don't believe me.

Puzzle Magic

Much of magic depends on misdirection—directing your audience to concentrate on the wrong thing while you pull off your hoax.

Here is a trick that looks like a real geometry problem. It fools most people because the lines and measurements misdirect the viewer's attention from the true solution to a fake one—at least for the short run.

Because a long look may give away the secret, there is a time limit. You have one minute to solve this before you look up the answer, which is to be found under the disguise of Magi-Climax 9 on page 124.

Here is the problem: X is the center of a circle. The line BC is five inches long and AB is nine and one-half inches long. Find the length of the diameter of the circle. Remember —only one minute for this one!

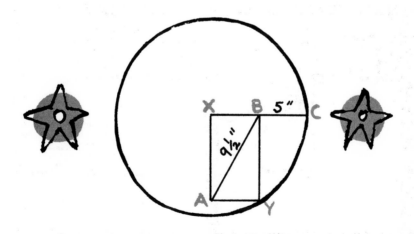

Exchequer

Did you know that in ancient times all the bookkeeping for the English treasury was recorded on a checkered tablecloth? That is why—in case you've ever wondered—the treasurer of England is called "Chancellor of the Exchequer." He kept the record of all the money that came into the treasury and all that was paid out from it.

In this trick you will be the Chancellor of the Exchequer. You will need as many pennies as you can find—at least twelve. But if you don't have pennies, you can use paper clips for pennies.

You are going to move the pennies around on the checkered sections in the illustration on the opposite page. If you do this according to the directions I give you, you will find that no matter how many pennies you started with, I can tell far, far ahead—even before this book was published—exactly how many you will have left in the end. (And remember, I did not tell you how many to have in your treasury.) You don't believe it? Try it and see.

1. Place an equal number of pennies in each of the three sections of this tablecloth—A, B and C. You may use any number of pennies, but there must be at least four in each group. The number is up to you!

2. Take two pennies from space C and drop these on the pile in space B.

3. Take three pennies from space A and place these also on the pile in space B.

4. Count how much you now have in space C. Now remove the same number from space B and transfer them to either of the other two piles.

5. Take one penny from either pile A or C and place it in space B.

6. Place all the money in spaces A and C in your pocket.

7. Count how much you now have left in the pile in space B. Remember this sum and turn to Magi-Climax 10 on page 124.

The Squeeze Inn

Numbers can be made to work the impossible! This is a story of how number magic was put to work to gain an extra room in a crowded inn. It's fantastic and fun! Here is the tale!

A group of nine weary travelers once arrived at a wayside inn and asked for rooms. Each wanted a private room. The manager, however, had to admit that he had only EIGHT rooms to offer them.

But as luck would have it, a magician overheard their problem and offered the following solution. He took the first traveler and one of the other nine and asked them both to stay in the first room for a few moments. Thus there were two men in this room temporarily.

He then asked the third man to go to the second room, the fourth to the third room, the fifth to the fourth room, the sixth to the fifth room, the seventh to the sixth room and the eighth to the seventh room.

This left one room vacant. So he returned to the first room and took the extra man away, leaving only one man in that room. He then led this extra, ninth man, who had been the temporary roommate of the occupant of room one, to the now empty extra room.

And so—once again—with a little number wizardry, the impossible came to pass. NINE men in EIGHT rooms, and no two men in a single room!

Magi-Climaxes

Magi-Climaxes

MAGI-CLIMAX 1

Did you say five thousand after the last number? Better luck next time. You tripped over that stepping stone!

MAGI-CLIMAX 2

Almost certainly your phrase reads: A MAN, A PLAN, A CANAL—PANAMA. At the most you will be one word off! Now, by the way, the letters of these seven words spell the same thing either way. It's a magic about face. Try it.

P.S. There IS a town, Trinidad, in Bolivia, South America, as well as in the West Indies!

P.P.S. "A atlas" is bad grammar!

MAGI-CLIMAX 3

If you are still trying to find the ZIG-ZAG LADY, back track to where your "book" is opened at pages five and six. Now, fold pages five and six back, as though folding from cover to cover, and then open again from the center.

MAGI-CLIMAX 4

It is my personal feeling that TEN is an extremely odd number of lumps of sugar to have in one cup. If you suggested to a friend that he have a cup of tea with ten lumps of sugar, he would think you were very odd indeed.

MAGI-CLIMAX 5

Amazing as it may seem, ninety-nine out of every hundred people who try this psychomagic trick will not only have three matches left but will also choose the box in the illustration below that contains three matches.

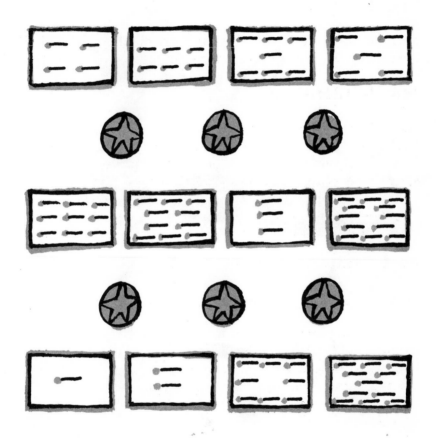

P.S. Should you be that one person in a hundred, I am sure that you did meet with half-success. If you did not have three matches left, you DID choose the box containing three matches, or vice-versa! Correct?

MAGI-CLIMAX 6

I have a hunch that we both share the same lucky charm. It really is a FISHY BUSINESS, this magic!

MAGI-CLIMAX 7

The first "psychological-numerical impression" I obtained from looking at this arrangement of cards was of a "one" and a "three." But since thirteen is unlucky, your total must be 31!

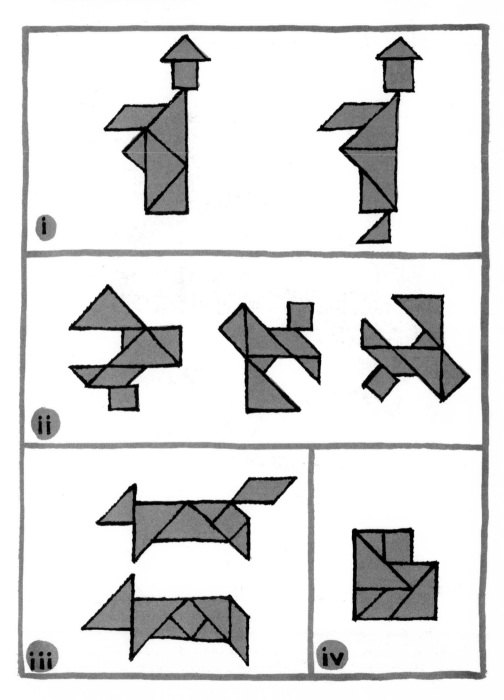

MAGI-CLIMAX 9

The answer is nineteen inches. The puzzle itself is not half as difficult as it looks. All you had to do was draw in the other diagonal of the rectangle BXAY. This diagonal is the radius of the circle. Since the radius of a circle is half its diameter, the answer is nine and one-half multiplied by two, or nineteen inches. That five-inch length BC was sheer misdirection! And as I'm sure you have noticed, misdirection is the essence of much magic.

MAGI-CLIMAX 10

If you placed in your three original equal piles the amount of money I think you did, you now have eight pennies left in the exchequer!

A Cure for Insomnia

When I was young, I used to spend many sleepless nights trying to figure out just how some of the almost impossible tricks of stage and television magicians worked. I would lie awake puzzling over these things. Finally, a cure for insomnia was needed. Counting rabbits jumping out of a hat was of no more use than counting sheep prancing over a fence. Then a glass of hot milk was suggested. However, I did not happen to like milk, so I had to resort to magic to save the day.

If you have trouble sleeping because some of the tricks in this book have you bamboozled, I will now share with you my magical cure for such insomnia.

You'll need these things: a milk bottle or other transparent jar; two teaspoons of citric acid crystals, which you can buy in a drugstore (or use the juice of a lemon) and about a tablespoon of bicarbonate of soda. No doubt you will find this in your mother's cupboard. Bicarbonate of soda is baking SODA, not baking POWDER. Also have on hand about five or six mothballs and some water.

Pour about a pint of water into the quart bottle or jar. Then add either the citric acid crystals or the lemon juice. Stir well. Now add the baking soda. It will froth up gloriously. While it is foaming, drop the mothballs into the liquid. Within a few minutes you will see these heavy balls float UP mysteriously from the bottom of the bottle and then DOWN again. They will go up and down, up and down, for an almost indefinite period. (From time to time you may want to shake the bottle a little.)

I promise you that if you spend five to ten minutes watching these "snowballs" rise and sink in their mystical way, your eyes will finally feel so tired that you will fall asleep as easily as you say, "Mothballs," "Magic," and "Goodnight."

"And now for my last trick . . ."

THE
SENTENCE
ON THE
OTHER
SIDE
OF
THIS
PAGE
IS
TRUE

THE
SENTENCE
ON THE
OTHER
SIDE
OF
THIS
PAGE
IS
FALSE